Working Papers for use with

**Fundamental Accounting Principles,
Chapters 1-6**

*By Kermit D. Larson
Paul B. W. Miller*

**For Seneca College
School of Business Management**

IRWIN
CUSTOM PUBLISHING
Burr Ridge, Illinois
Boston, Massachusetts
Sydney, Australia

Chapters were selected from:

Volume I Working Papers for use with Fundamental Accounting Principles, Thirteenth Edition
by Kermit D. Larson, Paul B. W. Miller. Copyright © Richard D. Irwin, Inc., 1987, 1990, and 1993.

©RICHARD D. IRWIN, INC., 1993

ISBN 0-256-18356-2

All rights reserved. No part of this publication may be reproduced, stored in a retrieval system, or transmitted, in any form or by any means, electronic, mechanical, photocopying, recording, or otherwise, without the prior written permission of the publisher.

Printed in the United States of America.

1 2 3 4 5 6 7 8 9 0 WCB 0 9 8 7 6 5 4

Contents

Chapter 1 1
Chapter 2 29
Chapter 3 73
Chapter 4 127
Chapter 5 205
Chapter 6 263

CHAPTER 1 EXERCISE 1-1   Name _____
Part 1

Part 2

EXERCISE 1-2

CHAPTER 1   EXERCISE 1-3

EXERCISE 1-4

EXERCISE 1-5

CHAPTER 1   EXERCISE 1-6   Name _____

a. _____

b. _____

c. _____

d. _____

CHAPTER 1   EXERCISE 1-7

	CASH	+	ACCOUNTS RECEIVABLE	+	MEDICAL EQUIPMENT	=	ACCOUNTS PAYABLE	+	IRINA ORMAN, CAPITAL	EXPLANATION
(a)	$15,700				$3,500				19,200	
(b)	(2,500)								rent (2,500)	
+/.	13,200				3500				16,700	
(c)					7600		7,600			
+/.	13,200				11,100		7,600		16,700	
(d)	260								revenue 260	
+/.	13,460				11,100		7,600		16,960	
(e)			2,800						rev. 2800	
+/.	13,460		2,800		11,100		7,600		19,760	
(f)	(590)				590					
+/.	12,870		2,800		11,690		7,600		19,760	
(g)	(1,900)								wages exp. 1,900	
+/.	10,970		2,800		11,690		7,600		17,860	
(h)	2,000		(2,000)							
+/.	12,970		800		11,690		7,600		17,860	
(i)	(7,600)						(7,600)			
+/.	5,370		800		11,690		0		17,860	

CHAPTER 1   **EXERCISE 1-8**   Name _____

EXERCISE 1-9

CHAPTER 1   EXERCISE 1-10

EXERCISE 1-11

CHAPTER 1 EXERCISE 1-12   Name _____

EXERCISE 1-13

CHAPTER 1 PROBLEM 1-1 or 1-1A Name _____
Parts 1 and 2

ASSETS					=	LIABILITIES		+	OWNER'S EQUITY	
CASH	ACCOUNTS RECEIVABLE	OFFICE SUPPLIES	OFFICE EQUIPMENT	BUILDING		ACCOUNTS PAYABLE	NOTES PAYABLE		CAPITAL	EXPLANATION OF CHANGE

Working Papers, Chapter 1

CHAPTER 1 PROBLEM 1-2 or 1-2A
Parts 1, 2 and 3

DATE	CASH	+	ACCOUNTS RECEIVABLE	+	PREPAID INSURANCE	+	SUPPLIES	=	ACCOUNTS PAYABLE	+	ISAAC TROW, CAPITAL	EXPLANATION OF CHANGE
July 1	5,600										5,600	INVESTMENT
1	(1,000)										(1,000)	
1	(120)						120					
3	(175)										(175)	
6	450										450	
9			1,275								1,275	
16	(925)										(925)	
19	1,275		(1,275)									
21			1,750								1,750	
22			1,200				200		200			
24			(1,750)						220		(220)	
28	1,750											
29					2,100						(2,100)	
30	(200)										(200)	
31	(150)										(150)	
31	(125)										(125)	
31	(825)										(825)	
31	(2,100)				2,100							
31	(1,000)										(1,000)	
Balance	3,555		1,200		2,100		320		420		5,755	
TTL (2)	6175						6175				6175	

CHAPTER 1   PROBLEM 1-2 or 1-2A (Continued)
Part 4

CHAPTER 1 PROBLEM 1-2 or 1-2A (Concluded)   Name
Part 5

Part 6

CHAPTER 1 PROBLEM 1-3 or 1-3A Name _____

Part 1

CHAPTER 1 PROBLEM 1-3 or 1-3A (Concluded)
Part 2

CHAPTER 1 PROBLEM 1-4 or 1-4A Name _____
Parts 1 and 2

DATE	CASH	+ ACCOUNTS RECEIVABLE	+ OFFICE SUPPLIES	+ PROFESSIONAL LIBRARY	+ OFFICE EQUIPMENT	= ACCOUNTS PAYABLE	+ CAPITAL	EXPLANATION OF CHANGE

ASSETS · LIABILITIES · OWNER'S EQUITY

CHAPTER 1 PROBLEM 1–4 or 1–4A (Continued)
Part 3

Part 4

CHAPTER 1 PROBLEM 1-4 or 1-4A (Concluded) Name _____
Part 5

CHAPTER 1   **PROBLEM 1-5 or 1-5A**   Name _____
Part 1

Part 2

CHAPTER 1 PROBLEM 1-5 or 1-5A (Concluded)
Part 3

Part 4

Part 5

CHAPTER 1   PROBLEM 1-6 or 1-6A   Name _____

TRANSACTION	BALANCE SHEET			INCOME STATE.	STATEMENT OF CASH FLOWS		
	TOTAL ASSETS	TOTAL LIAB.	EQUITY	NET INCOME	OPERATING	FINANCING	INVESTING
1.							
2.							
3.							
4.							
5.							
6.							
7.							
8.							
9.							
10.							
11.							
12.							
13.							
14.							

CHAPTER 1   PROBLEM 1–7 or 1–7A   Name _____

CHAPTER 1   PROBLEM 1-7 or 1-7A (Concluded)

CHAPTER 1   PROBLEM 1-8 or 1-8A   Name _____

CHAPTER 1   **PROBLEM 1-8 or 1-8A (Concluded)**

CHAPTER 2   EXERCISE 2-1

KIND OF ACCOUNT	INCREASES	DECREASES	NORMAL BALANCES
Asset	Debit	Credit	Debit
Liability	Credit	Debit	Credit
Owner's capital	Credit	Debit	Credit
Owner's withdrawals	Debit	Credit	Debit
Revenue	Credit	Debit	Credit
Expense	Debit	Credit	Debit

EXERCISE 2-2

a) Credit
b) Debit
c) Credit
d) Credit
e) Debit
f) Credit
g) Debit
h) Credit
j) Debit

EXERCISE 2-3

EXERCISE 2-4

Cash
a) 3,500 | 90 b)
d) 500 | 2800 e)
h) 200 | 60 g)
$1250

Accounts Receivable
f) 400 | 200 h)
$200

Office Supplies
b) 90
$90

Office Equipment
c) 2,800
$2,800

Accounts Payable
e) 2,800 | 2,800 c)
0

J. J. Wright, Capital
| 3,500 a)
| $3,500

Services Revenue
| 500 d)
| 400 f)
| $900

Utilities Expense
g) 60
$60

CHAPTER 2   **EXERCISE 2-5**

EXERCISE 2-6

ERROR	AMOUNT OUT OF BALANCE	COLUMN HAVING LARGER TOTAL

EXERCISE 2-7

CHAPTER 2   EXERCISE 2-8

Name _____

EXERCISE 2-9
Part 1

Part 2

Part 3

Working Papers, Chapter 2

CHAPTER 2   EXERCISE 2-10

EXERCISE 2-11

GENERAL JOURNAL   Page 1

DATE	ACCOUNT TITLES AND EXPLANATION	P.R.	DEBIT	CREDIT
Mar 1.	Cash		5000 —	
	Automobile		35000 —	
	TOM WATTS, Capital			40000 —
	invested money & car into limousine service			
1	Prepaid Rent		1200 —	
	Cash			1200 —
	paid rented office space 6 months in advanced.			
2.	Office equipment		900 —	
	Cash			900 —
	purchased phone for limo			
15.	Cash		2500 —	
	Fees Earned			2500 —
	collected fees earned			
31	Gas & Oil expense		260 —	
	Cash			260 —
	paid expense in full			

CHAPTER 2   EXERCISE 2-12
Parts 1 and 2

Name _____

```
       Cash                              Equipment
_____          _____
          |                                 |
          |                                 |
          |                                 |
          |                                 |
          |                                 |
          |                       _____
          |                         Tom Waits, Capital
          |                                 |
          |                                 |
          |                                 |
    Prepaid Rent                         Fees Earned
_____      _____
          |                                 |
          |                                 |
          |                                 |
          |                                 |
    Automobiles                     Gas and Oil Expense
_____      _____
          |                                 |
          |                                 |
          |                                 |
```

Part 3

Working Papers, Chapter 2   33

CHAPTER 2   EXERCISE 2-13

GENERAL JOURNAL   Page 1

DATE	ACCOUNT TITLES AND EXPLANATION	P.R.	DEBIT	CREDIT

EXERCISE 2-14

GENERAL JOURNAL   Page 1

DATE	ACCOUNT TITLES AND EXPLANATION	P.R.	DEBIT	CREDIT

CHAPTER 2   PROBLEM 2-1 or 2-1A
Parts 1 and 2

Name: Joel Obien

Cash
a)	50,000	b)	43,500
		f)	800
g)	3,500	h)	450
m)	1,200	i)	480
		j)	1,000
		l)	800
		n)	1,800
	$5,970		

Accounts Receivable
k)	1,300	m)	1,300
	0		

Office Supplies
c)	480	
	$1,480	

Automobiles
d)	17,200	
	$17,200	

Office Equipment
a)	20,000	j)	200
e)	2,500		
j)	1,200		
	$23,500		

Building
b)	230,000	
	$230,000	

Land
b)	60,000	
	$60,000	

Accounts Payable
i)	480	c)	480
		e)	2,500
			$2,500

Long-Term Notes Payable
		b)	246,500

April Stewart, Capital
		a)	70,000
		d)	17,200
			$87,200

April Stewart, Withdrawals
n)	1,800	
	$1,800	

Advertising Fees Earned
		g)	3,500
			$3,500

Marketing Research Fees Earned
		k)	1,300
			1,300

Office Salaries Expense
f)	800	
l)	800	
	$1,600	

Advertising Expense
h)	450	
	$450	

CHAPTER 2   PROBLEM 2-1 or 2-1A (Concluded)
Part 3

Stewart Advertising
Trial Balance
(Current Date)

Account	Debit	Credit
Cash	5,970.00	
Office Supplies	480.00	
Automobiles	17,200.00	
Office Equipment	2,350.00	
Building	23,000.00	
Land	6,000.00	
Accounts Payable		2,500.00
Long-Term Note Payable		24,650.00
April Stewart, Capital		8,720.00
April Stewart, Withdrawals	1,800.00	
Advertising Fees Earned		3,500.00
Marketing Research Fees Earned		1,300.00
Office Salaries Expense	1,600.00	
Advertising Expense	450.00	
TOTALS:	34,100.00	34,100.00

CHAPTER 2   PROBLEM 2-2 or 2-2A pg. 109   Name _____
Parts 1 and 2

Cash				Land		
a)	20,000	b)	3,800	b)	19,000	
e)	800	c)	8,000			
k)	2,100	d)	4,800			
		f)	700			
		l)	840			
		m)	250			
		n)	350			
		o)	260			
		p)	880			
		q)	150			
	$2,870					

Accounts Payable			
m)	250	h)	250
		j)	150
			150

Accounts Receivable				Alan Meaken, Capital		
g)	2,100	k)	2,100			a) 68,000
i)	3,150					
	3,150					

Long-Term Notes Payable		
	b)	15,200
	f)	3,000
		18,200

Prepaid Insurance		Alan Meaken, Withdrawals	
d) 4,800		o) 260	

Office Equipment		Surveying Fees Earned	
a) 3,000		e)	800
f)		g)	2,100
h) 250		i)	3,150
3,250			6,050

Surveying Equipment		Wages Expense	
a) 45,000		l) 840	
p) 3,700		p) 880	
48,700		1,720	

Building		Machinery Rental Expense	
c) 8,000		j) 150	

Working Papers, Chapter 2   37

CHAPTER 2 PROBLEM 2-2 or 2-2A (Concluded)

Permits Expense		Repairs Expense, Surveying Equipment	
g) 150		n) 350	

Part 2

Alan Meaken, Surveyor
Trial Balance
(current date)

Account	Debit	Credit
Cash	$2,870	
Accounts Receivable	3,150	
Prepaid Insurance	4,800	
Office Equipment	3,250	
Surveying "	4,870	
Building	8,000	
Land	19,000	
Accounts Payable		150
Long-Term Notes Pay.		18,200
Alan Meaken, Capital		6,8000
" Drawings	260	
Surveying Fees Earned		6,050
Wages Expense	1,720	
Machinery Rental Expense	150	
Permits Expense	150	
Repairs Expense, Surveying Equipment	350	
TOTALS:	92,400	92,400

CHAPTER 2   PROBLEM 2-3 or 2-3A   Name _____
Part 2

GENERAL JOURNAL   Page 1

DATE	ACCOUNT TITLES AND EXPLANATION	P.R.	DEBIT	CREDIT

Working Papers, Chapter 2

CHAPTER 2   PROBLEM 2-3 or 2-3A (Continued)

DATE	ACCOUNT TITLES AND EXPLANATION	P.R.	DEBIT	CREDIT

CHAPTER 2 PROBLEM 2-3 or 2-3A (Continued) Name _____
Parts 1 and 3

GENERAL LEDGER

Cash — Account No. 101

DATE	EXPLANATION	P.R.	DEBIT	CREDIT	BALANCE

Accounts Receivable — Account No. 106

DATE	EXPLANATION	P.R.	DEBIT	CREDIT	BALANCE

Office Supplies — Account No. 124

DATE	EXPLANATION	P.R.	DEBIT	CREDIT	BALANCE

Prepaid Insurance — Account No. 128

DATE	EXPLANATION	P.R.	DEBIT	CREDIT	BALANCE

Working Papers, Chapter 2

CHAPTER 2   PROBLEM 2-3 or 2-3A (Continued)

Prepaid Rent   Account No. 131

DATE	EXPLANATION	P.R.	DEBIT	CREDIT	BALANCE

Office Equipment   Account No. 163

DATE	EXPLANATION	P.R.	DEBIT	CREDIT	BALANCE

Accounts Payable   Account No. 201

DATE	EXPLANATION	P.R.	DEBIT	CREDIT	BALANCE

Kay Martinez, Capital   Account No. 301

DATE	EXPLANATION	P.R.	DEBIT	CREDIT	BALANCE

Kay Martinez, Withdrawals   Account No. 302

DATE	EXPLANATION	P.R.	DEBIT	CREDIT	BALANCE

CHAPTER 2   PROBLEM 2-3 or 2-3A (Concluded)   Name _____

Accounting Fees Earned — Account No. 401

DATE	EXPLANATION	P.R.	DEBIT	CREDIT	BALANCE

Utilities Expense — Account No. 690

DATE	EXPLANATION	P.R.	DEBIT	CREDIT	BALANCE

Part 4

CHAPTER 2 PROBLEM 2-4 or 2-4A pg. 111
Part 2

GENERAL JOURNAL — Page 1

DATE	ACCOUNT TITLES AND EXPLANATION	P.R.	DEBIT	CREDIT
Apr. 1	Cash	101	25000 —	
	Supplies	126	700 —	
	Office + Drafting Equipment	169	18500 —	
	Mike Leaman, Capital	301		44200 —
	began engineering firm			
1	Prepaid Rent	131	3100 —	
	Cash	101		3100 —
	prepaid two months rent			
3	Prepaid Insurance	128	2400 —	
	Cash	101		2400 —
	prepaid insurance.			
4	Drafting Equipment	120	680	
	Drafting Supplies	122	90	
	Accounts Payable	201		770 —
	purchased equipment + supplies on credit			
9	Cash	101	4000 —	
	Engineering Fees Earned	501		4000 —
	collected fees earned.			
15	Wages Expense	401	960 —	
	Cash	101		960 —
	paid wages.			
16	Accounts Receivable	110	7800 —	
	Engineering Fees Earned.	501		7800 —
	billed client on account.			
18	Drafting Supplies		40 —	
	Accounts Pay.			40 —
	purchased drafting supplies.			
19	Accounts Payable		770 —	
	Cash			770 —
	paid for equipment + supplies.			

Working Papers, Chapter 2

CHAPTER 2   PROBLEM 2-4 or 2-4A (Continued)

Page 2

DATE	ACCOUNT TITLES AND EXPLANATION	P.R.	DEBIT	CREDIT
Apr. 26	Cash		7800 —	
	Accounts Receivable			7800 —
	received payment in full			
27	Mike Leaman, Withdrawals		2000 —	
	Cash			2000 —
	withdrew money for personal use			
28	Accounts Payable		40 —	
	Cash			40 —
	paid for supplies purchased			
29	Accounts Receivable		1400 —	
	Engineering Fees Earned			1400 —
	completed work for clients			
30	Wages Expense		960 —	
	Cash			960 —
	paid salary			
30	Utilities Expense		170 —	
	Cash			170 —
	paid utilities			
30	Blueprinting Expense		110 —	
	Cash			110 —
	paid for blueprints expense			

CHAPTER 2   PROBLEM 2-4 or 2-4A (Continued)   Name _____
Parts 1 and 2

GENERAL LEDGER

Cash — Account No. 101

DATE	EXPLANATION	P.R.	DEBIT	CREDIT	BALANCE	
Apr. 1		1	25,000 —		25,000 —	DR
1		1		3,100 —	21,900 —	DR
3		1		2,400 —	19,500 —	DR
9		1	4,000 —		23,500 —	DR
15		1		960 —	22,540 —	DR
19		1		770 —	21,770 —	DR
26		2	7,800 —		29,570 —	DR
27		2		2,000 —	27,570 —	DR
28		2		40 —	27,530 —	DR
30		2		960 —	26,570 —	DR
30		2		170 —	26,400 —	DR
30		2		110 —	26,290 —	DR

Accounts Receivable — Account No. 106

DATE	EXPLANATION	P.R.	DEBIT	CREDIT	BALANCE	
Apr. 16		1	7,800 —		7,800 —	DR
26		2		7,800 —	0	
29		2	1,400 —		1,400 —	DR

Drafting Supplies — Account No. 126

DATE	EXPLANATION	P.R.	DEBIT	CREDIT	BALANCE	
Apr. 1		1	700 —		700 —	DR
4		1	90 —		790 —	DR
18		1	40 —		830 —	DR

Prepaid Insurance — Account No. 128

DATE	EXPLANATION	P.R.	DEBIT	CREDIT	BALANCE	
Apr. 3		1	2,400 —		2,400 —	DR

CHAPTER 2   PROBLEM 2-4 or 2-4A (Continued)

Prepaid Rent — Account No. 131

DATE	EXPLANATION	P.R.	DEBIT	CREDIT	BALANCE	
Apr. 1		1	3100 —		3100 —	DR

Office and Drafting Equipment — Account No. 167

DATE	EXPLANATION	P.R.	DEBIT	CREDIT	BALANCE	
Apr. 1		1	18500 —		18500 —	DR
4		1	680 —		19180 —	

Accounts Payable — Account No. 201

DATE	EXPLANATION	P.R.	DEBIT	CREDIT	BALANCE	
Apr. 4		1		770 —	770 —	CR
18		1		40 —	810 —	CR
19		1	770 —		40 —	CR
28		2	40 —		0	

Mike Leaman, Capital — Account No. 301

DATE	EXPLANATION	P.R.	DEBIT	CREDIT	BALANCE	
Apr. 1		1		44200 —	44200 —	CR

Mike Leaman, Withdrawals — Account No. 302

DATE	EXPLANATION	P.R.	DEBIT	CREDIT	BALANCE	
Apr. 27		2		2000 —	2000 —	CR

CHAPTER 2   PROBLEM 2-4 or 2-4A (Continued)   Name _____

Engineering Fees Earned Account No. 401

DATE	EXPLANATION	P.R.	DEBIT	CREDIT	BALANCE	
Apr. 9		1		4000 —	4000 —	CR
16		1		7800 —	11800 —	CR
29		2		1400 —	13200 —	CR

Salaries Expense Account No. 622

DATE	EXPLANATION	P.R.	DEBIT	CREDIT	BALANCE	
Apr. 15		1	960 —		960 —	DR
30		2	960 —		1920 —	DR

Blueprinting Expense Account No. 657

DATE	EXPLANATION	P.R.	DEBIT	CREDIT	BALANCE	
Apr. 30		2	110 —		110 —	DR

Utilities Expense Account No. 690

DATE	EXPLANATION	P.R.	DEBIT	CREDIT	BALANCE	
Apr. 30		2	170 —		170 —	DR

CHAPTER 2   PROBLEM 2-4 or 2-4A (Concluded)
Part 2

Mike Leaman, Engineer
Trial Balance
April 30, '19

Account	Debit	Credit
Cash	$26,290 —	
Accounts Receivable	1,400 —	
Drafting Supplies	830 —	
Prepaid Insurance	2,400 —	
Prepaid Rent	3,600 —	
Office & Drafting Equipment	19,180 —	
Accounts Payable		0
Mike Leaman, Capital		44,200 —
Mike Leaman, Withdrawal	2,000 —	
Engineering Fees Earned		13,200 —
Salaries Expense	1,920 —	
Blueprinting Expense	110 —	
Utilities Expense	170 —	
TOTAL:	57,400 —	57,400 —

CHAPTER 2   **PROBLEM 2-6 or 2-6A**   Name _____

CHAPTER 2   **PROBLEM 2-6 or 2-6A (Concluded)**

CHAPTER 2   PROBLEM 2-7 or 2-7A   Name _____

CHAPTER 2   **PROBLEM 2-7 or 2-7A (Concluded)**

SERIAL PROBLEM
Precision Computer Services

GENERAL JOURNAL   Page 1

DATE	ACCOUNT TITLES AND EXPLANATION	P.R.	DEBIT	CREDIT

SERIAL PROBLEM
Precision Computer Services (Continued)

Page 2

DATE	ACCOUNT TITLES AND EXPLANATION	P.R.	DEBIT	CREDIT

SERIAL PROBLEM
Precision Computer Services (Continued)

Name _____

Page 3

DATE	ACCOUNT TITLES AND EXPLANATION	P.R.	DEBIT	CREDIT

SERIAL PROBLEM
Precision Computer Services (Continued)

Page 4

DATE	ACCOUNT TITLES AND EXPLANATION	P.R.	DEBIT	CREDIT

SERIAL PROBLEM
Precision Computer Services (Continued)

Page 5

DATE	ACCOUNT TITLES AND EXPLANATION	P.R.	DEBIT	CREDIT

SERIAL PROBLEM
Precision Computer Services (Continued)

GENERAL LEDGER

Cash — Account No. 101

DATE	EXPLANATION	P.R.	DEBIT	CREDIT	BALANCE

SERIAL PROBLEM
Precision Computer Services (Continued)

Name _____

Accounts Receivable — Account No. 106

DATE	EXPLANATION	P.R.	DEBIT	CREDIT	BALANCE

Computer Supplies — Account No. 126

DATE	EXPLANATION	P.R.	DEBIT	CREDIT	BALANCE

Prepaid Insurance — Account No. 128

DATE	EXPLANATION	P.R.	DEBIT	CREDIT	BALANCE

Prepaid Rent — Account No. 131

DATE	EXPLANATION	P.R.	DEBIT	CREDIT	BALANCE

SERIAL PROBLEM
Precision Computer Services (Continued)

	Office Equipment			Account No. 163
DATE	EXPLANATION	P.R.	DEBIT	CREDIT	BALANCE

	Computer Equipment			Account No. 167
DATE	EXPLANATION	P.R.	DEBIT	CREDIT	BALANCE

	Accounts Payable			Account No. 201
DATE	EXPLANATION	P.R.	DEBIT	CREDIT	BALANCE

	John Conard, Capital			Account No. 301
DATE	EXPLANATION	P.R.	DEBIT	CREDIT	BALANCE

	John Conard, Withdrawals			Account No. 302
DATE	EXPLANATION	P.R.	DEBIT	CREDIT	BALANCE

SERIAL PROBLEM
Precision Computer Services (Continued)

Computer Services Revenue — Account No. 403

DATE	EXPLANATION	P.R.	DEBIT	CREDIT	BALANCE

Wages Expense — Account No. 623

DATE	EXPLANATION	P.R.	DEBIT	CREDIT	BALANCE

Advertising Expense — Account No. 655

DATE	EXPLANATION	P.R.	DEBIT	CREDIT	BALANCE

Mileage Expense — Account No. 676

DATE	EXPLANATION	P.R.	DEBIT	CREDIT	BALANCE

SERIAL PROBLEM
Precision Computer Services (Concluded)

Miscellaneous Expenses — Account No. 677

DATE	EXPLANATION	P.R.	DEBIT	CREDIT	BALANCE

Repairs Expense, Computer — Account No. 684

DATE	EXPLANATION	P.R.	DEBIT	CREDIT	BALANCE

Telephone Expense — Account No. 688

DATE	EXPLANATION	P.R.	DEBIT	CREDIT	BALANCE

Utilities Expense — Account No. 690

DATE	EXPLANATION	P.R.	DEBIT	CREDIT	BALANCE

CHAPTER 3　　EXERCISE 3-1

Name _____

GENERAL JOURNAL　　　　　　　　　　　　　　Page 1

DATE	ACCOUNT TITLES AND EXPLANATION	P.R.	DEBIT	CREDIT

EXERCISE 3-2

GENERAL JOURNAL　　　　　　　　　　　　　　Page 1

	DATE	ACCOUNT TITLES AND EXPLANATION	P.R.	DEBIT	CREDIT
a)	Dec. 30	Supplies expense		700 —	
		Supplies			700 —
		to expense supplies used			
b)	31	Insurance Expense		1360 —	
		Prepaid Insurance			1360 —
		to expense insurance used			
c)	31	Insurance Expense		200 —	
		Prepaid Insurance			200 —
		to expense Insurance used.			

EXERCISE 3-3

_____
_____
_____
_____
_____
_____
_____
_____

EXERCISE 3-4

_____
_____
_____
_____

Working Papers, Chapter 3

CHAPTER 3   EXERCISE 3-5

GENERAL JOURNAL   Page 1

DATE	ACCOUNT TITLES AND EXPLANATION	P.R.	DEBIT	CREDIT

EXERCISE 3-6

CHAPTER 3 EXERCISE 3-7

GENERAL JOURNAL
Page 1

DATE	ACCOUNT TITLES AND EXPLANATION	P.R.	DEBIT	CREDIT

EXERCISE 3-8

			DEBIT	CREDIT
Anthony Joseph, Capital December 31, 1993				
Investments Owner			56350 —	
Net Income			41000 —	
Total:				97350 —
Less: Withdrawals				47000 —
Anthony Joseph, Capital				50350 —

Working Papers, Chapter 3

CHAPTER 3   EXERCISE 3-8 (Concluded)

Anthony Joseph, Photographer
Balance Sheet
December 31, 1993

Current Assets:			
Cash		$6,700	
Accounts Receivable		4,100	
Photography Supplies		1,950	
Prepaid Insurance		2,050	
Total Current Assets			$14,800
Investments:			
Investment in Geffen Corporation common shares		2,200	
Total Investments			2,200
Fixed Assets:			
Photography Equipment	42,400		
Less accumulated amortization	20,750	21,650	
Building	85,000		
Less accumulated Amortization	31,600	53,400	
Land		70,000	
Total capital assets			$145,050
Total Assets:			$162,050
Liabilities			
Current Liabilities			
Salaries payable	$400		
Unearned photography Fees	2,800		
Total Current Liabilities		3,200	
Long-Term Liabilities			
Long-Term notes payable		108,500	
Total Liabilities			$111,700
Owner's Equity			
Anthony Joseph, Capital			50,350
Total Liabilities & Owner's Equity			$162,050

CHAPTER 3   EXERCISE 3-9   Name _____

GENERAL JOURNAL   Page 1

DATE	ACCOUNT TITLES AND EXPLANATION	P.R.	DEBIT	CREDIT

EXERCISE 3-10

EXERCISE 3-11

Working Papers, Chapter 3

CHAPTER 3   EXERCISE 3-12

EXERCISE 3-13

GENERAL JOURNAL — Page 1

DATE	ACCOUNT TITLES AND EXPLANATION	P.R.	DEBIT	CREDIT

EXERCISE 3-14

GENERAL JOURNAL — Page 1

DATE	ACCOUNT TITLES AND EXPLANATION	P.R.	DEBIT	CREDIT

CHAPTER 3 PROBLEM 3-1 or 3-1A
Part 1

GENERAL JOURNAL — Page 1

	DATE	ACCOUNT TITLES AND EXPLANATION	P.R.	DEBIT	CREDIT
a)	Dec. 31	Office Supplies Expense		430 —	
		Office Supplies			430 —
		to record supplies expense used			
b)	31	Insurance Expense		900 —	
		Prepaid Insurance (2900/360)x12			900 —
		to record expired insurance			
	31	Insurance Expense (3480/24)x10		1450 —	
		Prepaid Insurance			1450 —
		to record expired insurance			
	31	Insurance Expense (540/12)x6		270 —	
		Prepaid Insurance			270 —
		to record expired insurance			
c)	31	Wages Expense		1000 —	
		Wages Payable			1000 —
		to accrue wages for last 3 days of the year.			
	Jan. 1	Wages Expense		250 —	
		Wages Payable		1000 —	
		Cash			1250 —
		to pay week's salary.			

Working Papers, Chapter 3

CHAPTER 3   PROBLEM 3-1 or 3-1A (Concluded)
Part 2

GENERAL JOURNAL   Page 2

DATE	ACCOUNT TITLES AND EXPLANATION	P.R.	DEBIT	CREDIT

CHAPTER 3 PROBLEM 3-2 or 3-2A
Part 2

GENERAL JOURNAL Page 1

	DATE	ACCOUNT TITLES AND EXPLANATION	P.R.	DEBIT	CREDIT
a)	Dec. 31	Insurance Expense	637	900 —	
		Prepaid Insurance	128		900 —
b)	31	Office Supplies Expense	650	2630 —	
		Office Supplies	124		2630 —
		(4,300 – 1,670)			
c)	31	Amortization Expense, Equipment	612	3300 —	
		Accumulated Amort. Equipment	168		3300 —
d)	31	Amortization Expense, Prof. Library	614	1320 —	
		Accumulated Amort. Prof. Library	158		1320 —
e)	31	Salaries Expense (70 × 3)	622	210 —	
		Salaries Payable	209		210 —

Working Papers, Chapter 3

CHAPTER 3   PROBLEM 3-2 or 3-2A (Continued)
Parts 1 and 2

GENERAL LEDGER

Cash — Account No. 101

DATE	EXPLANATION	P.R.	DEBIT	CREDIT	BALANCE
Dec. 31	Balance	√			7 200 00

Accounts Receivable — Account No. 106

DATE	EXPLANATION	P.R.	DEBIT	CREDIT	BALANCE

Office Supplies — Account No. 124

DATE	EXPLANATION	P.R.	DEBIT	CREDIT	BALANCE
Dec. 31	Balance	√			4 300 00

Prepaid Insurance — Account No. 128

DATE	EXPLANATION	P.R.	DEBIT	CREDIT	BALANCE
Dec. 31	Balance	√			8 100 00
				900 —	

Professional Library — Account No. 157

DATE	EXPLANATION	P.R	DEBIT	CREDIT	BALANCE
Dec. 31	Balance	√			19 800 00

CHAPTER 3 PROBLEM 3-2 or 3-2A (Continued) Name _____

Accumulated Depreciation, Professional Library Account No. 158

DATE	EXPLANATION	P.R.	DEBIT	CREDIT	BALANCE
Dec. 31	Balance	√			8,490 00

Equipment Account No. 167

DATE	EXPLANATION	P.R.	DEBIT	CREDIT	BALANCE
Dec. 31	Balance	√			43,300 00

Accumulated Depreciation, Equipment Account No. 168

DATE	EXPLANATION	P.R.	DEBIT	CREDIT	BALANCE
Dec. 31	Balance	√			14,900 00

Accounts Payable Account No. 201

DATE	EXPLANATION	P.R.	DEBIT	CREDIT	BALANCE
Dec. 31	Balance	√			860 00

Salaries Payable Account No. 209

DATE	EXPLANATION	P.R.	DEBIT	CREDIT	BALANCE

Unearned Extension Fees Account No. 233

DATE	EXPLANATION	P.R.	DEBIT	CREDIT	BALANCE
Dec. 31	Balance	√			2,400 00

CHAPTER 3   PROBLEM 3-2 or 3-2A (Continued)

Kay Perry, Capital — Account No. 301

DATE	EXPLANATION	P.R.	DEBIT	CREDIT	BALANCE
Dec. 31	Balance	√			55 950 00

Kay Perry, Withdrawals — Account No. 302

DATE	EXPLANATION	P.R.	DEBIT	CREDIT	BALANCE
Dec. 31	Balance	√			15 000 00

Enrollment Fees Earned — Account No. 401

DATE	EXPLANATION	P.R.	DEBIT	CREDIT	BALANCE
Dec. 31	Balance	√			43 400 00

Extension Fees Earned — Account No. 402

DATE	EXPLANATION	P.R.	DEBIT	CREDIT	BALANCE

Depreciation Expense, Equipment — Account No. 612

DATE	EXPLANATION	P.R.	DEBIT	CREDIT	BALANCE

Depreciation Expense, Professional Library — Account No. 614

DATE	EXPLANATION	P.R.	DEBIT	CREDIT	BALANCE

CHAPTER 3   PROBLEM 3-2 or 3-2A (Continued)   Name _____

Salaries Expense — Account No. 622

DATE	EXPLANATION	P.R.	DEBIT	CREDIT	BALANCE
Dec. 31	Balance	√			16,800.00

Insurance Expense — Account No. 637

DATE	EXPLANATION	P.R.	DEBIT	CREDIT	BALANCE
Dec. 31			900 —		900 — DR

Rent Expense — Account No. 640

DATE	EXPLANATION	P.R.	DEBIT	CREDIT	BALANCE
Dec. 31	Balance	√			9,600.00

Office Supplies Expense — Account No. 650

DATE	EXPLANATION	P.R.	DEBIT	CREDIT	BALANCE

Advertising Expense — Account No. 655

DATE	EXPLANATION	P.R.	DEBIT	CREDIT	BALANCE
Dec. 31	Balance	√			500.00

Utilities Expense — Account No. 690

DATE	EXPLANATION	P.R.	DEBIT	CREDIT	BALANCE
Dec. 31	Balance	√			1,400.00

CHAPTER 3 PROBLEM 3-2 or 3-2A (Continued)
Part 3

CHAPTER 3 PROBLEM 3-2 or 3-2A (Continued) Name _____

CHAPTER 3   PROBLEM 3-2 or 3-2A (Concluded)

CHAPTER 3 PROBLEM 3-3 or 3-3A
Part 1

GENERAL JOURNAL — Page 1

	DATE	ACCOUNT TITLES AND EXPLANATION	P.R.	DEBIT	CREDIT
a)	Dec. 31	Insurance Expense	637	2220 —	
		Prepaid Insurance	128		2220 —
b)	Dec. 31	Landscape Supplies Expense	652	1270 —	
		Landscape Supplies	126		1270 —
c)	Dec. 31	Amortization Expense, Landscaping Equipment	612	820 —	
		Accumulated Amort., Landscaping Equipment	168		820 —
d)	Dec. 31	Amortization Expense, Trucks	611	6600 —	
		Accumulated Amort., Trucks	154		6600 —
e)	Dec. 31	Amortization Expense, Building	606	3020 —	
		Accumulated Amort., Building	154		3020 —
f)	Dec. 31	Unearned Landscape Architecture Fees	233	750 —	
		Landscape Architecture Fees Earned	401		750 —
g)	Dec. 31	Accounts Receivable	106	480 —	
		Landscape Architecture Fees Earned	401		480 —
h)	Dec. 31	Landscape Wages Expense	623	630 —	
		Wages Payable	210		630 —

Working Papers, Chapter 3

CHAPTER 3 PROBLEM 3-3 or 3-3A (Continued)

GENERAL LEDGER

Cash — Account No. 101

DATE	EXPLANATION	P.R.	DEBIT	CREDIT	BALANCE
Dec. 31	Balance	√			3000 00

Accounts Receivable — Account No. 106

DATE	EXPLANATION	P.R.	DEBIT	CREDIT	BALANCE
Dec. 31	Balance	√			1400 00
				480 —	1880 —

Landscaping Supplies — Account No. 126

DATE	EXPLANATION	P.R.	DEBIT	CREDIT	BALANCE
Dec. 31	Balance	√			1680 00
				1270 —	410 —

Prepaid Insurance — Account No. 128

DATE	EXPLANATION	P.R.	DEBIT	CREDIT	BALANCE
Dec. 31	Balance	√			3200 00
				2220 —	980 —

Investment in Sierra, Inc., Common Stock — Account No. 141

DATE	EXPLANATION	P.R.	DEBIT	CREDIT	BALANCE
Dec. 31	Balance	√			6000 00

Trucks — Account No. 153

DATE	EXPLANATION	P.R.	DEBIT	CREDIT	BALANCE
Dec. 31	Balance	√			42000 00

CHAPTER 3   PROBLEM 3-3 or 3-3A (Continued)   Name _____

Accumulated Depreciation, Trucks — Account No. 154

DATE	EXPLANATION	P.R.	DEBIT	CREDIT	BALANCE
Dec. 31	Balance	√			17 000 00
			6 600 —		10 400 —

Landscaping Equipment — Account No. 167

DATE	EXPLANATION	P.R.	DEBIT	CREDIT	BALANCE
Dec. 31	Balance	√			5 700 00

Accumulated Depreciation, Landscaping Equipment — Account No. 168

DATE	EXPLANATION	P.R.	DEBIT	CREDIT	BALANCE
Dec. 31	Balance	√			1 900 00
			820 —		1 080 —

Building — Account No. 173

DATE	EXPLANATION	P.R.	DEBIT	CREDIT	BALANCE
Dec. 31	Balance	√			68 000 00

Accumulated Depreciation, Building — Account No. 174

DATE	EXPLANATION	P.R.	DEBIT	CREDIT	BALANCE
Dec. 31	Balance	√			19 800 00
			3 020 —		16 780 —

Land — Account No. 183

DATE	EXPLANATION	P.R.	DEBIT	CREDIT	BALANCE
Dec. 31	Balance	√			16 000 00

CHAPTER 3   PROBLEM 3-3 or 3-3A (Continued)

Franchise — Account No. 193

DATE	EXPLANATION	P.R.	DEBIT	CREDIT	BALANCE
Dec. 31	Balance	√			30 000 00

Wages Payable — Account No. 210

DATE	EXPLANATION	P.R.	DEBIT	CREDIT	BALANCE
Dec. 31				630—	630—

Unearned Landscape Architecture Fees — Account No. 233

DATE	EXPLANATION	P.R.	DEBIT	CREDIT	BALANCE
Dec. 31	Balance	√			1 050 00
			750		300—

Long-Term Notes Payable — Account No. 251

DATE	EXPLANATION	P.R.	DEBIT	CREDIT	BALANCE
Dec. 31	Balance	√			75 600 00

Eve Adams, Capital — Account No. 301

DATE	EXPLANATION	P.R.	DEBIT	CREDIT	BALANCE
Dec. 31	Balance	√			49 270 00

Eve Adams, Withdrawals — Account No. 302

DATE	EXPLANATION	P.R.	DEBIT	CREDIT	BALANCE
Dec. 31	Balance	√			27 000 00

CHAPTER 3 PROBLEM 3-3 or 3-3A (Continued)   Name _____

Landscape Architecture Fees Earned — Account No. 401

DATE	EXPLANATION	P.R.	DEBIT	CREDIT	BALANCE
Dec. 31	Balance	√			12,250.00
				750—	13,000—
				480	13,480—

Landscape Services Revenue — Account No. 403

DATE	EXPLANATION	P.R.	DEBIT	CREDIT	BALANCE
Dec. 31	Balance	√			84,000.00

Depreciation Expense, Building — Account No. 606

DATE	EXPLANATION	P.R.	DEBIT	CREDIT	BALANCE
Dec. 31			3020—		3020—

Depreciation Expense, Trucks — Account No. 611

DATE	EXPLANATION	P.R.	DEBIT	CREDIT	BALANCE
			6600—		6600—

Depreciation Expense, Landscaping Equipment — Account No. 612

DATE	EXPLANATION	P.R.	DEBIT	CREDIT	BALANCE
			820—		820—

Office Salaries Expense — Account No. 620

DATE	EXPLANATION	P.R.	DEBIT	CREDIT	BALANCE
Dec. 31	Balance	√			14,200.00

CHAPTER 3   PROBLEM 3-3 or 3-3A (Continued)

Landscape Wages Expense — Account No. 623

DATE	EXPLANATION	P.R.	DEBIT	CREDIT	BALANCE
Dec. 31	Balance	√			31,950.00
			630—		32,580—

Interest Expense — Account No. 633

DATE	EXPLANATION	P.R.	DEBIT	CREDIT	BALANCE
Dec. 31	Balance	√			6,800.00

Insurance Expense — Account No. 637

DATE	EXPLANATION	P.R.	DEBIT	CREDIT	BALANCE
			2,220—		2,220—

Landscaping Supplies Expense — Account No. 652

DATE	EXPLANATION	P.R.	DEBIT	CREDIT	BALANCE
			1,270—		1,270—

Gas, Oil, and Repairs Expense — Account No. 669

DATE	EXPLANATION	P.R.	DEBIT	CREDIT	BALANCE
Dec. 31	Balance	√			3,940.00

CHAPTER 3　PROBLEM 3-3 or 3-3A (Continued)
Part 2

EDEN's GARDEN
Adjusted Trial Balance
December 31, 1993

Account	Debit	Credit
Cash	3000 —	
A/R	1880 —	
Landscaping Supplies	410 —	
Ppd. Insurance	980 —	
Investment	6000 —	
Trucks	42000 —	
Accumulated Amortization, trucks		23600 —
Landscaping Equipment	5700 —	
Accumulated Amort. Landscaping Equip.		2720 —
Building	68000 —	
Accumulated Amort. Building		22820 —
Land	16000 —	
Franchise	3000 —	
Wages Payable		630 —
Unearned Landscaping Architecture Fees		300 —
Long-terms notes payable		75600 —
Eve Adams, Capital		49270 —
" " withdrawals	27000 —	
Landscaping Architecture Fees earned		13480 —
" " Services Revenue		84000 —
Amortization Expense, building	3020 —	
" " trucks	6600 —	
" " landscaping equip.	820 —	
Office Salaries Expense	14200 —	
Landscaping Wages	32580 —	
Interest Expense	6800 —	
Insurance "	2220 —	
Landscaping Supplies Exp.	1270 —	
Gas, Oil, + repairs Exp.	3940 —	
Totals:	272420 —	272420 —

Working Papers, Chapter 3

CHAPTER 3   PROBLEM 3-3 or 3-3A (Continued)

For the Year Ended December 31, 1993

Revenues:			
	$13,480 —		
	84,000 —		
		$97,480 —	
Operating Expenses:			
		71,450 —	
Net Income		$26,030 —	

Eve Adam's Capital,		39,290 —	
Plus			
Owner's Investments	12,000 —		
Net Income	26,030 —	38,030 —	
Totals		77,320 —	
Less: Withdrawals		27,000 —	
Eve Adams, capital, December 31, 1993		$48,300 —	

CHAPTER 3 PROBLEM 3-3 or 3-3A (Concluded)

Eden's Garden
Classified Balance Sheet
December 31, 1993

CHAPTER 3 PROBLEM 3-4 or 3-4A
Part 2

Name _____

GENERAL JOURNAL
Page 1

DATE	ACCOUNT TITLES AND EXPLANATION	P.R.	DEBIT	CREDIT

CHAPTER 3   PROBLEM 3-4 or 3-4A (Continued)
Parts 1 and 3

GENERAL LEDGER

Cash — Account No. 101

DATE	EXPLANATION	P.R.	DEBIT	CREDIT	BALANCE
Dec. 31	Balance	√			2 850 00

Accounts Receivable — Account No. 106

DATE	EXPLANATION	P.R.	DEBIT	CREDIT	BALANCE

Office Supplies — Account No. 124

DATE	EXPLANATION	P.R.	DEBIT	CREDIT	BALANCE
Dec. 31	Balance	√			1 800 00

Prepaid Insurance — Account No. 128

DATE	EXPLANATION	P.R.	DEBIT	CREDIT	BALANCE
Dec. 31	Balance	√			1 470 00

Office Equipment — Account No. 163

DATE	EXPLANATION	P.R.	DEBIT	CREDIT	BALANCE
Dec. 31	Balance	√			3 400 00

Accumulated Depreciation, Office Equipment — Account No. 164

DATE	EXPLANATION	P.R.	DEBIT	CREDIT	BALANCE
Dec. 31	Balance	√			2 300 00

CHAPTER 3   PROBLEM 3-4 or 3-4A (Continued)   Name _____

Buildings   Account No. 173

DATE	EXPLANATION	P.R.	DEBIT	CREDIT	BALANCE
Dec. 31	Balance	√			174500 00

Accumulated Depreciation, Buildings   Account No. 174

DATE	EXPLANATION	P.R.	DEBIT	CREDIT	BALANCE
Dec. 31	Balance	√			28750 00

Land   Account No. 183

DATE	EXPLANATION	P.R.	DEBIT	CREDIT	BALANCE
Dec. 31	Balance	√			48000 00

Interest Payable   Account No. 203

DATE	EXPLANATION	P.R.	DEBIT	CREDIT	BALANCE

Wages Payable   Account No. 210

DATE	EXPLANATION	P.R.	DEBIT	CREDIT	BALANCE

Estimated Property Taxes Payable   Account No. 213

DATE	EXPLANATION	P.R.	DEBIT	CREDIT	BALANCE

CHAPTER 3   PROBLEM 3-4 or 3-4A (Continued)

Unearned Fees — Account No. 233

DATE	EXPLANATION	P.R.	DEBIT	CREDIT	BALANCE
Dec. 31	Balance	√			1,300.00

Long-Term Notes Payable — Account No. 251

DATE	EXPLANATION	P.R.	DEBIT	CREDIT	BALANCE
Dec. 31	Balance	√			155,750.00

John Eagle, Capital — Account No. 301

DATE	EXPLANATION	P.R.	DEBIT	CREDIT	BALANCE
Dec. 31	Balance	√			30,260.00

John Eagle, Withdrawals — Account No. 302

DATE	EXPLANATION	P.R.	DEBIT	CREDIT	BALANCE
Dec. 31	Balance	√			12,000.00

Fees Earned — Account No. 401

DATE	EXPLANATION	P.R.	DEBIT	CREDIT	BALANCE
Dec. 31	Balance	√			51,640.00

Depreciation Expense, Buildings — Account No. 606

DATE	EXPLANATION	P.R.	DEBIT	CREDIT	BALANCE

CHAPTER 3   PROBLEM 3–4 or 3–4A (Continued)   Name _____

Depreciation Expense, Office Equipment — Account No. 612

DATE	EXPLANATION	P.R.	DEBIT	CREDIT	BALANCE

Wages Expense — Account No. 623

DATE	EXPLANATION	P.R.	DEBIT	CREDIT	BALANCE
Dec. 31	Balance	√			8 700 00

Interest Expense — Account No. 633

DATE	EXPLANATION	P.R.	DEBIT	CREDIT	BALANCE
Dec. 31	Balance	√			13 470 00

Insurance Expense — Account No. 637

DATE	EXPLANATION	P.R.	DEBIT	CREDIT	BALANCE

Office Supplies Expense — Account No. 650

DATE	EXPLANATION	P.R.	DEBIT	CREDIT	BALANCE

Property Taxes Expense — Account No. 683

DATE	EXPLANATION	P.R.	DEBIT	CREDIT	BALANCE
Dec. 31	Balance	√			3 100 00

Working Papers, Chapter 3

CHAPTER 3   PROBLEM 3-4 or 3-4A (Continued)

	Utilities Expense				Account No. 690
DATE	EXPLANATION	P.R.	DEBIT	CREDIT	BALANCE
Dec. 31	Balance	√			2 3 3 0 00

Part 3

CHAPTER 3 PROBLEM 3-4 or 3-4A (Continued)

CHAPTER 3 PROBLEM 3-4 or 3-4A (Concluded)

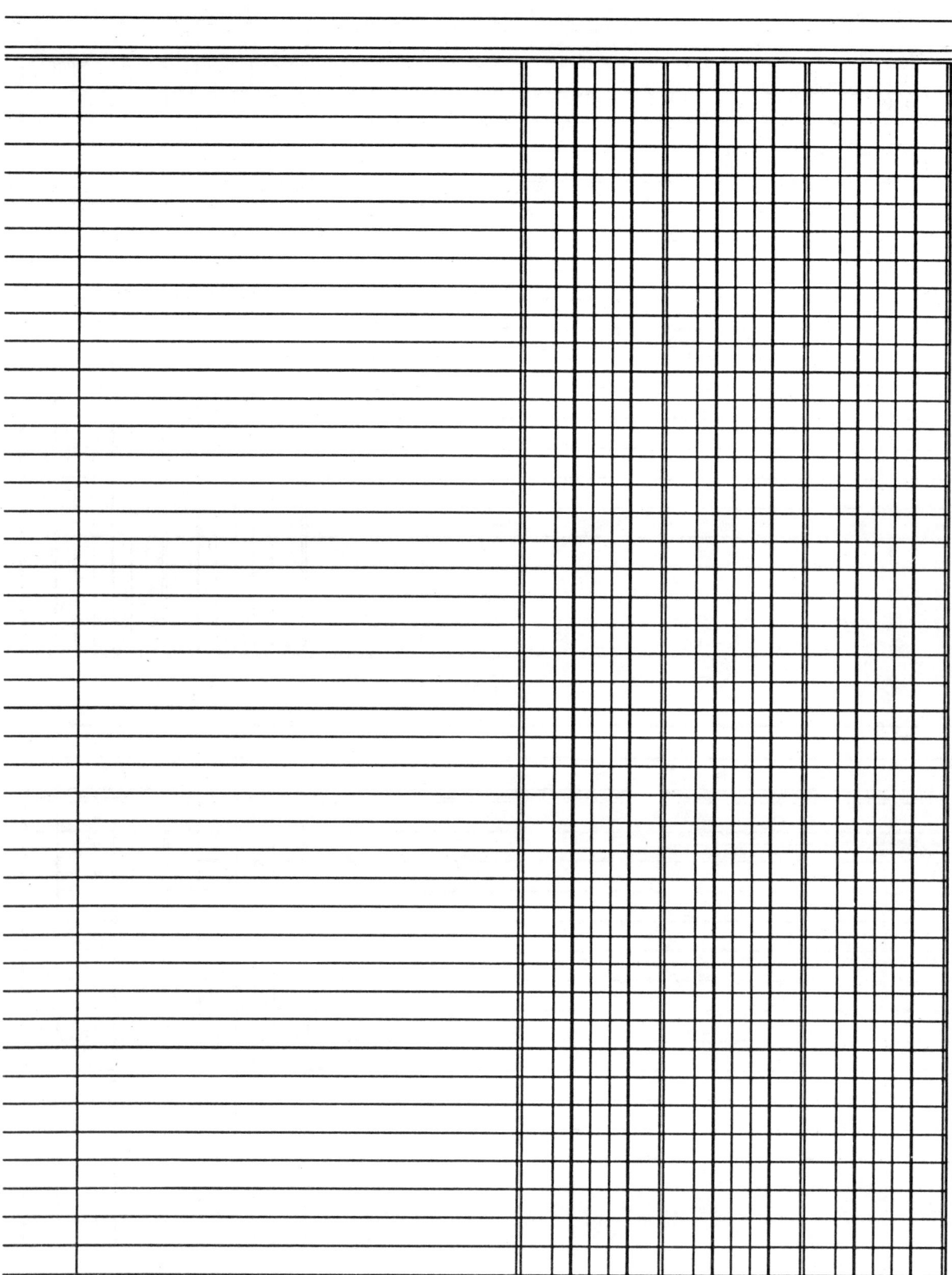

CHAPTER 3   PROBLEM 3-5 or 3-5A   Name _____

GENERAL JOURNAL   Page 1

DATE	ACCOUNT TITLES AND EXPLANATION	P.R.	DEBIT	CREDIT

GENERAL JOURNAL

DATE	ACCOUNT TITLES AND EXPLANATION	P.R.	DEBIT	CREDIT

CHAPTER 3   PROBLEM 3-6 or 3-6A   Name _____

CHAPTER 3   PROBLEM 3-6 or 3-6A (Concluded)

CHAPTER 3   PROBLEM 3-7 or 3-7A   Name _____

GENERAL JOURNAL   Page 1

DATE	ACCOUNT TITLES AND EXPLANATION	P.R.	DEBIT	CREDIT

CHAPTER 3   PROBLEM 3-8 or 3-8A   Name _____

CHAPTER 3   PROBLEM 3-8 or 3-8A (Concluded)

CHAPTER 3 PROBLEM 3-9 or 3-9A Name _____

CHAPTER 3   **PROBLEM 3-9 or 3-9A (Concluded)**

SERIAL PROBLEM
Precision Computer Services
Part 1

GENERAL JOURNAL — Page 6

DATE	ACCOUNT TITLES AND EXPLANATION	P.R.	DEBIT	CREDIT

Working Papers, Chapter 3

SERIAL PROBLEM
Precision Computer Services (Continued)

DATE	ACCOUNT TITLES AND EXPLANATION	P.R.	DEBIT	CREDIT

SERIAL PROBLEM
Precision Computer Services (Continued)

GENERAL LEDGER

Cash — Account No. 101

DATE	EXPLANATION	P.R.	DEBIT	CREDIT	BALANCE
1993 Nov. 30	Balance				3,110.00

Accounts Receivable — Account No. 106

DATE	EXPLANATION	P.R.	DEBIT	CREDIT	BALANCE
1993 Nov. 30	Balance				2,620.00

Computer Supplies — Account No. 126

DATE	EXPLANATION	P.R.	DEBIT	CREDIT	BALANCE
1993 Nov. 30	Balance				150.00

Prepaid Insurance — Account No. 128

DATE	EXPLANATION	P.R.	DEBIT	CREDIT	BALANCE
1993 Nov. 30	Balance				195.00

SERIAL PROBLEM
Precision Computer Services (Continued)

	Prepaid Rent				Account No. 131
DATE	EXPLANATION	P.R.	DEBIT	CREDIT	BALANCE
1993 Nov. 30	Balance				900 00

	Office Equipment				Account No. 163
DATE	EXPLANATION	P.R.	DEBIT	CREDIT	BALANCE
1993 Nov. 30	Balance				340 00

	Accumulated Depreciation, Office Equipment				Account No. 164
DATE	EXPLANATION	P.R.	DEBIT	CREDIT	BALANCE

	Computer Equipment				Account No. 167
DATE	EXPLANATION	P.R.	DEBIT	CREDIT	BALANCE
1993 Nov. 30	Balance				3,000 00

	Accumulated Depreciation, Computer Equipment				Account No. 168
DATE	EXPLANATION	P.R.	DEBIT	CREDIT	BALANCE

	Accounts Payable				Account No. 201
DATE	EXPLANATION	P.R.	DEBIT	CREDIT	BALANCE
1993 Nov. 30	Balance				-0-

SERIAL PROBLEM
Precision Computer Services (Continued)

Wages Payable — Account No. 210

DATE	EXPLANATION	P.R.	DEBIT	CREDIT	BALANCE

Unearned Computer Fees — Account No. 233

DATE	EXPLANATION	P.R.	DEBIT	CREDIT	BALANCE

John Conard, Capital — Account No. 301

DATE	EXPLANATION	P.R.	DEBIT	CREDIT	BALANCE
1993 Nov. 30	Balance				8 340 00

John Conard, Withdrawals — Account No. 302

DATE	EXPLANATION	P.R.	DEBIT	CREDIT	BALANCE
1993 Nov. 30	Balance				2 485 00

Computer Services Revenue — Account No. 403

DATE	EXPLANATION	P.R.	DEBIT	CREDIT	BALANCE
1993 Nov. 30	Balance				6 345 00

Depreciation Expense, Office Equipment — Account No. 612

DATE	EXPLANATION	P.R.	DEBIT	CREDIT	BALANCE

SERIAL PROBLEM
Precision Computer Services (Continued)

Depreciation Expense, Computer Equipment — Account No. 613

DATE	EXPLANATION	P.R.	DEBIT	CREDIT	BALANCE

Wages Expense — Account No. 623

DATE	EXPLANATION	P.R.	DEBIT	CREDIT	BALANCE
1993 Nov. 30	Balance				1 190 00

Insurance Expense — Account No. 637

DATE	EXPLANATION	P.R.	DEBIT	CREDIT	BALANCE

Rent Expense — Account No. 640

DATE	EXPLANATION	P.R.	DEBIT	CREDIT	BALANCE

Computer Supplies Expense — Account No. 652

DATE	EXPLANATION	P.R.	DEBIT	CREDIT	BALANCE

Advertising Expense — Account No. 655

DATE	EXPLANATION	P.R.	DEBIT	CREDIT	BALANCE
1993 Nov. 30	Balance				15 00

SERIAL PROBLEM
Precision Computer Services (Continued)

Name _____

Mileage Expense — Account No. 676

DATE	EXPLANATION	P.R.	DEBIT	CREDIT	BALANCE
1993 Nov. 30	Balance				312 00

Miscellaneous Expenses — Account No. 677

DATE	EXPLANATION	P.R.	DEBIT	CREDIT	BALANCE
1993 Nov. 30	Balance				14 00

Repairs Expense, Computer — Account No. 684

DATE	EXPLANATION	P.R.	DEBIT	CREDIT	BALANCE
1993 Nov. 30	Balance				25 00

Telephone Expense — Account No. 688

DATE	EXPLANATION	P.R.	DEBIT	CREDIT	BALANCE
1993 Nov. 30	Balance				233 00

Utilities Expense — Account No. 690

DATE	EXPLANATION	P.R.	DEBIT	CREDIT	BALANCE
1993 Nov. 30	Balance				96 00

SERIAL PROBLEM
Precision Computer Services (Continued)
Part 2

PRECISION COMPUTER SERVICES
Adjusted Trial Balance
December 31, 1993

SERIAL PROBLEM
Precision Computer Services (Continued)

Name _____

PRECISION COMPUTER SERVICES
Income Statement
For Quarter Ended December 31, 1993

PRECISION COMPUTER SERVICES
Statement of Changes in Owner's Equity
For Quarter Ended December 31, 1993

SERIAL PROBLEM
Precision Computer Services (Concluded)

PRECISION COMPUTER SERVICES
Balance Sheet
December 31, 1993

CHAPTER 4   EXERCISE 4-1 pj.218   Name _____

EXERCISE 4-2

GENERAL JOURNAL   Page 1

DATE	ACCOUNT TITLES AND EXPLANATION	P.R.	DEBIT	CREDIT

CHAPTER 4   EXERCISE 4-3 pg. 214

Rita Ivy, Capital		Rent Expense
31 22,500	Dec. 31 19,700	Dec. 31 5,400 5,400
	31 15,125	

Rita Ivy, Withdrawals		Salaries Expense
Dec 31 22,500	22,500	Dec. 31 4,200 4,200

Income Summary		Supplies Expense
31 22,975	38,100	Dec. 31 9,775 9,775
31 15,125	31 15,125	

Fees Earned		Depreciation Expense, Equipment
31 38,100	Dec. 31 38,100	Dec. 31 3,600 3,600

GENERAL JOURNAL   Page 1

DATE	ACCOUNT TITLES AND EXPLANATION	P.R.	DEBIT	CREDIT
	Income Summary		22,975	
	Expenses			22,975
	Sales		38,100	
	Income Summary			38,100
	Income Summary		15,125	
	Capital			15,125
	Capital A/c		22,500	
	W/drawals			22,500

CHAPTER 4   EXERCISE 4-4 pg. 215   Name _____

GENERAL JOURNAL   Page 1

DATE	ACCOUNT TITLES AND EXPLANATION	P.R.	DEBIT	CREDIT
Dec. 31	Fees Earned		71000 —	
	Income Summary			71000 —
	(to close revenue)			
Dec. 31	Income Summary		33840 —	
	expenses (individually)			33840 —
	(to close expenses)			
Dec. 31	Income Summary		37160 —	
	Capital			37160 —
	(to close income summary)			
Dec. 31	Capital A/c		32000 —	
	W/drawals			32000 —
	(to close withdrawals)			

EXERCISE 4-5

Common Stock

Retained Earnings

Income Summary

Services Revenue

Cash Dividends Declared

Rent Expense

Salaries Expense

Insurance Expense

Depreciation Expense, Equipment

Working Papers, Chapter 4

CHAPTER 4   EXERCISE 4-5 (Concluded)

GENERAL JOURNAL   Page 1

DATE	ACCOUNT TITLES AND EXPLANATION	P.R.	DEBIT	CREDIT

EXERCISE 4-6

GENERAL JOURNAL   Page 1

DATE	ACCOUNT TITLES AND EXPLANATION	P.R.	DEBIT	CREDIT

CHAPTER 4   EXERCISE 4-7
Parts 1 and 2

Cash		
a) 150,000	b) 146,500	
d) 27,000	e) 18,000	
	g) 7,500	
	h) 5,000	
	0	

Common Stock	
	a) 150,000

Retained Earnings (capital)	
iv) 7,500	iii) 12,000
	4,500

Accounts Receivable	
c) 30,000	d) 27,000
3,000	

Income Summary	
ii) 18,000	i) 30,000
iii) 12,000	12,000
	0

Equipment	
b) 146,500	
h) 12,000	
158,500	

Cash Dividends Declared (Drawings)	
f) 7,500	iv) 7,500
	0

Notes Payable	
	h) 7,000

Services Revenue	
i) 30,000	c) 30,000
	0

Common Dividend Payable	
g) 7,500	f) 7,500
	0

Operating Expenses	
e) 18,000	ii) 18,000
	0

Part 3

_____
_____
_____
_____
_____
_____
_____
_____
_____
_____
_____

CHAPTER 4   EXERCISE 4-8
Parts 1 and 2

WARE PRINTING COMPANY
Work Sheet
For Month Ended Current Date

ACCOUNT TITLES	TRIAL BALANCE DR.	TRIAL BALANCE CR.	ADJUSTMENTS DR.	ADJUSTMENTS CR.	ADJUSTED TRIAL BALANCE DR.	ADJUSTED TRIAL BALANCE CR.	INCOME STATEMENT DR.	INCOME STATEMENT CR.	STATEMENT OF CHANGES IN OWNER'S EQUITY OR BALANCE SHEET DR.	STATEMENT OF CHANGES IN OWNER'S EQUITY OR BALANCE SHEET CR.
Account Payable		2 —				2 —				2 —
Account Receivable	5 —				5 —				5 —	
Acc. Amor - Printing Equip		12 —		(a) 4 —		16 —				16 —
Cash	4 —				4 —				4 —	
Notes Payable		3 —				3 —				3 —
Prepaid Insurance	2 —			(b) 1 —	1 —				1 —	
Rent Expense	7 —				7 —		7 —			
Printing Services Revenue		24 —				24 —		24 —		
Ruby Ware, Capital		30 —				30 —				30 —
" " Withdrawals	8 —				8 —				8 —	
Printing Equipment	30 —				30 —				30 —	
Printing Supplies	6 —			(c) 3 —	3 —				3 —	
Wages Expense	9 —		(d) 1 —		10 —		10 —			
Total:	71 —	71 —								
Amortization Expense			(a) 4 —		4 —		4 —			
Insurance Expense			(b) 1 —		1 —		1 —			
Printing Supplies Expense			(c) 3 —		3 —		3 —			
Wages Payable				(d) 1 —		1 —				1 —
Totals:			9 —	9 —	76 —	76 —	25 —	24 —	51 —	52 —
Net loss								1 —	1 —	
							25 —	25 —	52 —	52 —

CHAPTER 4　　EXERCISE 4-13
Parts 1 and 2

Name _____

GENERAL JOURNAL   Page 1

DATE	ACCOUNT TITLES AND EXPLANATION	P.R.	DEBIT	CREDIT

CHAPTER 4   PROBLEM 4-1 or 4-1A   Name _____

(The work sheet for this problem is in the back of this booklet.)

Part 2

GENERAL JOURNAL   Page 1

DATE	ACCOUNT TITLES AND EXPLANATION	P.R.	DEBIT	CREDIT
	Insurance Expense		1410—	
	Prepaid Insurance			1410—
	Office Supplies Exp.		640—	
	Office Supplies			640—
	Amortization Expense		2800—	
	Accumulated Amortization			2800—
	Wages Expense		220—	
	Wages Payable			220—

Working Papers, Chapter 4

CHAPTER 4   PROBLEM 4-1 or 4-1A (Continued)

Closing entries

Page 2

DATE	ACCOUNT TITLES AND EXPLANATION	P.R.	DEBIT	CREDIT
	Fees earned		5640000 —	
	Income Summary			5640000 —
	to close revenue account.			
	Income Summary		3194000 —	
	Wages Expense			1844000 —
	Rent "			750000 —
	Utilities "			115000 —
	Insurance "			141000 —
	Supplies "			6400
	Amortization " Office Equipment			280000
	to close expenses			
	Income Summary		2446000 —	
	Capital account			2446000 —
	to close income summary account.			
	Capital Account		2250000 —	
	Withdrawals			2250000 —

CHAPTER 4   PROBLEM 4-1 or 4-1A (Continued)
Part 3

Dunhill Employment Services
Income Statement
For the Year Ended December 31, 1993

Revenue:		
Employment Fees Earned		$56,400
Expenses:		
Wages Expense	$18,440	
Rent Expense	7,500	
Utilities Expense	1,150	
Insurance Expense	1,410	
Supplies Expense	640	
Amortization Office Equip.	2,800	
Total expenses:		$31,940
Net Income:		$24,460

B.K. Dunhill, capital, December 31, 1992		$16,380
Plus:		
Investments		
Net Income	24,460	24,460
Total		$40,840
Less Owner's withdrawals		22,500
B.K. Dunhill capital, December 31, 1993		$18,340

CHAPTER 4   PROBLEM 4-1 or 4-1A (Concluded)

Classified Balance Sheet

CHAPTER 4   PROBLEM 4-2 or 4-2A   Name _____
(The work sheet for this problem is in the back of this booklet.)
Parts 2 and 4

GENERAL JOURNAL
Page 1

DATE	ACCOUNT TITLES AND EXPLANATION	P.R.	DEBIT	CREDIT

Working Papers, Chapter 4

CHAPTER 4   PROBLEM 4-2 or 4-2A (Continued)

Page 2

DATE	ACCOUNT TITLES AND EXPLANATION	P.R.	DEBIT	CREDIT

CHAPTER 4   PROBLEM 4-2 or 4-2A (Continued)   Name _____

GENERAL LEDGER

Cash   Account No. 101

DATE	EXPLANATION	P.R.	DEBIT	CREDIT	BALANCE
Dec. 31	Balance	√			2,740.00

Surveying Supplies   Account No. 126

DATE	EXPLANATION	P.R.	DEBIT	CREDIT	BALANCE
Dec. 31	Balance	√			1,930.00

Prepaid Insurance   Account No. 128

DATE	EXPLANATION	P.R.	DEBIT	CREDIT	BALANCE
Dec. 31	Balance	√			3,500.00

Prepaid Interest   Account No. 129

DATE	EXPLANATION	P.R.	DEBIT	CREDIT	BALANCE

Surveying Equipment   Account No. 167

DATE	EXPLANATION	P.R.	DEBIT	CREDIT	BALANCE
Dec. 31	Balance	√			85,365.00

Working Papers, Chapter 4

CHAPTER 4   PROBLEM 4-2 or 4-2A (Continued)

Accumulated Depreciation, Surveying Equipment — Account No. 168

DATE	EXPLANATION	P.R.	DEBIT	CREDIT	BALANCE
Dec. 31	Balance	√			35 460 00

Accounts Payable — Account No. 201

DATE	EXPLANATION	P.R.	DEBIT	CREDIT	BALANCE
Dec. 31	Balance	√			900 00

Rent Payable — Account No. 208

DATE	EXPLANATION	P.R.	DEBIT	CREDIT	BALANCE

Wages Payable — Account No. 210

DATE	EXPLANATION	P.R.	DEBIT	CREDIT	BALANCE

Estimated Property Taxes Payable — Account No. 213

DATE	EXPLANATION	P.R.	DEBIT	CREDIT	BALANCE

CHAPTER 4   PROBLEM 4-2 or 4-2A (Continued)   Name _____

Long-Term Notes Payable — Account No. 251

DATE	EXPLANATION	P.R.	DEBIT	CREDIT	BALANCE
Dec. 31	Balance	√			12 000 00

Lisa Garza, Capital — Account No. 301

DATE	EXPLANATION	P.R.	DEBIT	CREDIT	BALANCE
Dec. 31	Balance	√			34 680 00

Lisa Garza, Withdrawals — Account No. 302

DATE	EXPLANATION	P.R.	DEBIT	CREDIT	BALANCE
Dec. 31	Balance	√			21 000 00

Surveying Fees Earned — Account No. 401

DATE	EXPLANATION	P.R.	DEBIT	CREDIT	BALANCE
Dec. 31	Balance	√			58 400 00

Depreciation Expense, Surveying Equipment — Account No. 612

DATE	EXPLANATION	P.R.	DEBIT	CREDIT	BALANCE

Working Papers, Chapter 4

CHAPTER 4   PROBLEM 4–2 or 4–2A (Continued)

Wages Expense — Account No. 623

DATE	EXPLANATION	P.R.	DEBIT	CREDIT	BALANCE
Dec. 31	Balance	√			16 820 00

Interest Expense — Account No. 633

DATE	EXPLANATION	P.R.	DEBIT	CREDIT	BALANCE
Dec. 31	Balance	√			720 00

Insurance Expense — Account No. 637

DATE	EXPLANATION	P.R.	DEBIT	CREDIT	BALANCE

Rent Expense — Account No. 640

DATE	EXPLANATION	P.R.	DEBIT	CREDIT	BALANCE
Dec. 31	Balance	√			5 400 00

Surveying Supplies Expense — Account No. 652

DATE	EXPLANATION	P.R.	DEBIT	CREDIT	BALANCE

CHAPTER 4   PROBLEM 4-2 or 4-2A (Continued)   Name _____

Property Taxes Expense — Account No. 683

DATE	EXPLANATION	P.R.	DEBIT	CREDIT	BALANCE
Dec. 31	Balance	√			2,470.00

Repairs Expense, Equipment — Account No. 684

DATE	EXPLANATION	P.R.	DEBIT	CREDIT	BALANCE
Dec. 31	Balance	√			535.00

Utilities Expense — Account No. 690

DATE	EXPLANATION	P.R.	DEBIT	CREDIT	BALANCE
Dec. 31	Balance	√			960.00

Income Summary — Account No. 901

DATE	EXPLANATION	P.R.	DEBIT	CREDIT	BALANCE

CHAPTER 4   PROBLEM 4-2 or 4-2A (Continued)
Part 3

MESA SURVEYING COMPANY
Income Statement
For Year Ended December 31, 1993

MESA SURVEYING COMPANY
Statement of Changes in Owner's Equity
For Year Ended December 31, 1993

CHAPTER 4 — PROBLEM 4-2 or 4-2A (Continued) Name _____

MESA SURVEYING COMPANY
Balance Sheet
December 31, 1993

CHAPTER 4 PROBLEM 4-2 or 4-2A (Concluded)
Part 4

MESA SURVEYING COMPANY
Post-Closing Trial Balance
December 31, 1993

CHAPTER 4   PROBLEM 4-3 or 4-3A   Name _____

(The work sheet for this problem is in the back of this booklet.)

Part 3

TOWER WINDOW CLEANING
Income Statement
For Year Ended December 31, 1993

Revenue:

TOWER WINDOW CLEANING
Statement of Changes in Owner's Equity
For Year Ended December 31, 1993

CHAPTER 4   PROBLEM 4-3 or 4-3A (Continued)

TOWER WINDOW CLEANING
Balance Sheet
December 31, 1993

CHAPTER 4 PROBLEM 4-3 or 4-3A (Continued)
Parts 2 and 4

GENERAL JOURNAL — Page 1

DATE	ACCOUNT TITLES AND EXPLANATION	P.R.	DEBIT	CREDIT
a)	Insurance Expense		1580 -	
	Prepaid Insurance			1580 -
b)	Cleaning Supplies Expense		205 -	
	Cleaning Supplies			205
c)	Amortization Expense		495 -	
	Acc. Amortization			495 -
d)	Amortization Expense		3650 -	
	Acc. Amortization			3650 -
e)				
f)	Acc. Rec.		125 -	
	Unearned Cleaning Revenue		600 -	
	Cleaning Service Revenue			725 -
g)				
h)	Office Salaries Expense		145 -	
	Salaries Payable			145 -
	Cleaning Wages Exp.		225 -	
	Cleaning Wages Payable			225 -

Working Papers, Chapter 4

CHAPTER 4   PROBLEM 4-3 or 4-3A (Continued)

Page 2

DATE	ACCOUNT TITLES AND EXPLANATION	P.R.	DEBIT	CREDIT
	Fees Earned Revenue			53575—
	Income Summary		53575—	
	to close revenue.			
	Income Summary			
	Office Salaries Exp.			

CHAPTER 4 PROBLEM 4-3 or 4-3A (Continued) Name _____

GENERAL LEDGER

Cash — Account No. 101

DATE	EXPLANATION	P.R.	DEBIT	CREDIT	BALANCE
Dec. 31	Balance	√			890 00

Accounts Receivable — Account No. 106

DATE	EXPLANATION	P.R.	DEBIT	CREDIT	BALANCE
Dec. 31	Balance	√			1400 00

Cleaning Supplies — Account No. 126

DATE	EXPLANATION	P.R.	DEBIT	CREDIT	BALANCE
Dec. 31	Balance	√			470 00

Prepaid Insurance — Account No. 128

DATE	EXPLANATION	P.R.	DEBIT	CREDIT	BALANCE
Dec. 31	Balance	√			2100 00

Prepaid Rent — Account No. 131

DATE	EXPLANATION	P.R.	DEBIT	CREDIT	BALANCE
Dec. 31	Balance	√			350 00

CHAPTER 4   PROBLEM 4-3 or 4-3A (Continued)

Trucks   Account No. 153

DATE	EXPLANATION	P.R.	DEBIT	CREDIT	BALANCE
Dec. 31	Balance	√			18,235.00

Accumulated Depreciation, Trucks   Account No. 154

DATE	EXPLANATION	P.R.	DEBIT	CREDIT	BALANCE
Dec. 31	Balance	√			7,295.00

Cleaning Equipment   Account No. 167

DATE	EXPLANATION	P.R.	DEBIT	CREDIT	BALANCE
Dec. 31	Balance	√			4,930.00

Accumulated Depreciation, Cleaning Equipment   Account No. 168

DATE	EXPLANATION	P.R.	DEBIT	CREDIT	BALANCE
Dec. 31	Balance	√			1,970.00

Accounts Payable   Account No. 201

DATE	EXPLANATION	P.R.	DEBIT	CREDIT	BALANCE
Dec. 31	Balance	√			985.00

CHAPTER 4 PROBLEM 4-3 or 4-3A (Continued) Name _____

Rent Payable — Account No. 208

DATE	EXPLANATION	P.R.	DEBIT	CREDIT	BALANCE

Salaries Payable — Account No. 209

DATE	EXPLANATION	P.R.	DEBIT	CREDIT	BALANCE

Wages Payable — Account No. 210

DATE	EXPLANATION	P.R.	DEBIT	CREDIT	BALANCE

Unearned Cleaning Services Revenue — Account No. 236

DATE	EXPLANATION	P.R.	DEBIT	CREDIT	BALANCE
Dec. 31	Balance	√			800 00

Marian Stone, Capital — Account No. 301

DATE	EXPLANATION	P.R.	DEBIT	CREDIT	BALANCE
Dec. 31	Balance	√			10 115 00

CHAPTER 4 PROBLEM 4-3 or 4-3A (Continued)

Marian Stone, Withdrawals — Account No. 302

DATE	EXPLANATION	P.R.	DEBIT	CREDIT	BALANCE
Dec. 31	Balance	√			15 000 00

Cleaning Services Revenue — Account No. 403

DATE	EXPLANATION	P.R.	DEBIT	CREDIT	BALANCE
Dec. 31	Balance	√			52 850 00

Depreciation Expense, Trucks — Account No. 611

DATE	EXPLANATION	P.R.	DEBIT	CREDIT	BALANCE

Depreciation Expense, Cleaning Equipment — Account No. 612

DATE	EXPLANATION	P.R.	DEBIT	CREDIT	BALANCE

Office Salaries Expense — Account No. 620

DATE	EXPLANATION	P.R.	DEBIT	CREDIT	BALANCE
Dec. 31	Balance	√			9 600 00

CHAPTER 4 PROBLEM 4-3 or 4-3A (Continued) Name _____

Cleaning Wages Expense — Account No. 623

DATE	EXPLANATION	P.R.	DEBIT	CREDIT	BALANCE
Dec. 31	Balance	√			15 840 00

Insurance Expense — Account No. 637

DATE	EXPLANATION	P.R.	DEBIT	CREDIT	BALANCE

Rent Expense — Account No. 640

DATE	EXPLANATION	P.R.	DEBIT	CREDIT	BALANCE
Dec. 31	Balance	√			3 500 00

Cleaning Supplies Expense — Account No. 652

DATE	EXPLANATION	P.R.	DEBIT	CREDIT	BALANCE

Gas, Oil, and Repairs Expense — Account No. 669

DATE	EXPLANATION	P.R.	DEBIT	CREDIT	BALANCE
Dec. 31	Balance	√			1 220 00

CHAPTER 4   PROBLEM 4-3 or 4-3A (Concluded)

Telephone Expense — Account No. 688

DATE	EXPLANATION	P.R.	DEBIT	CREDIT	BALANCE
Dec. 31	Balance	√			480 00

Income Summary — Account No. 901

DATE	EXPLANATION	P.R.	DEBIT	CREDIT	BALANCE

Part 4

TOWER WINDOW CLEANING
Post-Closing Trial Balance
December 31, 1993

Account	Debit	Credit
Cash		
A/R		
Cleaning Supplies		
Ppd. Insurance		
Trucks		
Cleaning Equip.		
Nancy Stone, Capital		
Totals	26365 —	26365 —

CHAPTER 4   PROBLEM 4-4 or 4-4A   Name _____
Parts 1, 2, 3 and 4

GENERAL JOURNAL   Page 1

DATE	ACCOUNT TITLES AND EXPLANATION	P.R.	DEBIT	CREDIT

Working Papers, Chapter 4

CHAPTER 4   PROBLEM 4-4 or 4-4A (Concluded)

Page 2

DATE	ACCOUNT TITLES AND EXPLANATION	P.R.	DEBIT	CREDIT

CHAPTER 4 PROBLEM 4-5 or 4-5A Name _____
Part 1

GENERAL JOURNAL   Page 1

DATE	ACCOUNT TITLES AND EXPLANATION	P.R.	DEBIT	CREDIT

CHAPTER 4 PROBLEM 4-5 or 4-5A (Concluded)
Part 2

GENERAL JOURNAL — Page 2

DATE	ACCOUNT TITLES AND EXPLANATION	P.R.	DEBIT	CREDIT

CHAPTER 4 PROBLEM 4-6 or 4-6A Name _____

GENERAL JOURNAL Page 1

DATE	ACCOUNT TITLES AND EXPLANATION	P.R.	DEBIT	CREDIT

CHAPTER 4   PROBLEM 4-6 or 4-6A (Continued)

Page 2

DATE	ACCOUNT TITLES AND EXPLANATION	P.R.	DEBIT	CREDIT

CHAPTER 4   PROBLEM 4-6 or 4-6A (Continued)   Name _____

Page 3

DATE	ACCOUNT TITLES AND EXPLANATION	P.R.	DEBIT	CREDIT

CHAPTER 4   PROBLEM 4-6 or 4-6A (Continued)

DATE	ACCOUNT TITLES AND EXPLANATION	P.R.	DEBIT	CREDIT

CHAPTER 4   PROBLEM 4-6 or 4-6A (Continued)   Name _____

GENERAL LEDGER

Cash — Account No. 101

DATE	EXPLANATION	P.R.	DEBIT	CREDIT	BALANCE

Office Supplies — Account No. 124

DATE	EXPLANATION	P.R.	DEBIT	CREDIT	BALANCE

Prepaid Insurance — Account No. 128

DATE	EXPLANATION	P.R.	DEBIT	CREDIT	BALANCE

CHAPTER 4   PROBLEM 4-6 or 4-6A (Continued)

Automobiles — Account No. 151

DATE	EXPLANATION	P.R.	DEBIT	CREDIT	BALANCE

Accumulated Depreciation, Automobiles — Account No. 152

DATE	EXPLANATION	P.R.	DEBIT	CREDIT	BALANCE

Salaries Payable — Account No. 209

DATE	EXPLANATION	P.R.	DEBIT	CREDIT	BALANCE

Ted Dey, Capital — Account No. 301

DATE	EXPLANATION	P.R.	DEBIT	CREDIT	BALANCE

Ted Dey, Withdrawals — Account No. 302

DATE	EXPLANATION	P.R.	DEBIT	CREDIT	BALANCE

Consulting Fees Earned — Account No. 401

DATE	EXPLANATION	P.R.	DEBIT	CREDIT	BALANCE

CHAPTER 4   PROBLEM 4-6 or 4-6A (Continued)   Name _____

Depreciation Expense, Automobiles   Account No. 605

DATE	EXPLANATION	P.R.	DEBIT	CREDIT	BALANCE

Salaries Expense   Account No. 622

DATE	EXPLANATION	P.R.	DEBIT	CREDIT	BALANCE

Insurance Expense   Account No. 637

DATE	EXPLANATION	P.R.	DEBIT	CREDIT	BALANCE

Rent Expense   Account No. 640

DATE	EXPLANATION	P.R.	DEBIT	CREDIT	BALANCE

CHAPTER 4 PROBLEM 4-6 or 4-6A (Continued)

Office Supplies					Account No. 650
DATE	EXPLANATION	P.R.	DEBIT	CREDIT	BALANCE

Gas, Oil, and Repairs Expense					Account No. 669
DATE	EXPLANATION	P.R.	DEBIT	CREDIT	BALANCE

Telephone Expense					Account No. 688
DATE	EXPLANATION	P.R.	DEBIT	CREDIT	BALANCE

Income Summary					Account No. 901
DATE	EXPLANATION	P.R.	DEBIT	CREDIT	BALANCE

CHAPTER 4   PROBLEM 4-6 or 4-6A (Continued)   Name _____

DEY FINANCIAL SERVICES
Work Sheet
For Month Ended June 30, 1993

ACCOUNT TITLES	UNADJUSTED TRIAL BALANCE		ADJUSTMENTS		ADJUSTED TRIAL BALANCE		INCOME STATEMENT		STATEMENT OF CHANGES IN OWNER'S EQUITY OR BALANCE SHEET	
	DR.	CR.	DR.	CR.	DR.	CR.	DR.	CR.	DR.	CR.
Cash										
Office supplies										
Prepaid insurance										
Automobiles										
Ted Dey, capital										
Consulting fees earned										
Salaries expense										
Rent expense										
Gas, oil, and repairs expense										
Telephone expense										

CHAPTER 4   PROBLEM 4-6 or 4-6A (Continued)

DEY FINANCIAL SERVICES
Work Sheet
For Month Ended July 31, 1993

ACCOUNT TITLES	UNADJUSTED TRIAL BALANCE DR.	CR.	ADJUSTMENTS DR.	CR.	ADJUSTED TRIAL BALANCE DR.	CR.	INCOME STATEMENT DR.	CR.	STATEMENT OF CHANGES IN OWNER'S EQUITY OR BALANCE SHEET DR.	CR.
Cash										
Office supplies										
Prepaid insurance										
Automobiles										
Accum. depr., automobiles										
Ted Dey, capital										
Ted Dey, withdrawals										
Consulting fees earned										
Salaries expense										
Rent expense										
Gas, oil, and repairs expense										
Telephone expense										

CHAPTER 4   PROBLEM 4-6 or 4-6A (Continued)   Name _____

DEY FINANCIAL SERVICES
Income Statement
For Month Ended June 30, 1993

DEY FINANCIAL SERVICES
Statement of Changes in Owner's Equity
For Month Ended June 30, 1993

CHAPTER 4 PROBLEM 4-6 or 4-6A (Continued)

DEY FINANCIAL SERVICES
Balance Sheet
June 30, 1993

DEY FINANCIAL SERVICES
Post-Closing Trial Balance
June 30, 1993

CHAPTER 4   PROBLEM 4-6 or 4-6A (Continued)   Name _____

DEY FINANCIAL SERVICES
Income Statement
For Month Ended July 31, 1993

DEY FINANCIAL SERVICES
Statement of Changes in Owner's Equity
For Month Ended July 31, 1993

CHAPTER 4   PROBLEM 4-6 or 4-6A (Concluded)

DEY FINANCIAL SERVICES
Balance Sheet
July 31, 1993

DEY FINANCIAL SERVICES
Post-Closing Trial Balance
July 31, 1993

CHAPTER 4   PROBLEM 4-7 or 4-7A   Name _____

CHAPTER 4   **PROBLEM 4-7 or 4-7A (Concluded)**

CHAPTER 4   **PROBLEM 4-8 or 4-8A**   Name _____

CHAPTER 4   PROBLEM 4–8 or 4–8A (Concluded)

SERIAL PROBLEM
Precision Computer Services

Name _____

GENERAL JOURNAL — Page 8

DATE	ACCOUNT TITLES AND EXPLANATION	P.R.	DEBIT	CREDIT

SERIAL PROBLEM
Precision Computer Services (Continued)

GENERAL LEDGER

Cash — Account No. 101

DATE	EXPLANATION	P.R.	DEBIT	CREDIT	BALANCE
1993 Dec. 31	Balance				4,410.00

Accounts Receivable — Account No. 106

DATE	EXPLANATION	P.R.	DEBIT	CREDIT	BALANCE
1993 Dec. 31	Balance				670.00

Computer Supplies — Account No. 126

DATE	EXPLANATION	P.R.	DEBIT	CREDIT	BALANCE
1993 Dec. 31	Balance				17.00

Prepaid Insurance — Account No. 128

DATE	EXPLANATION	P.R.	DEBIT	CREDIT	BALANCE
1993 Dec. 31	Balance				1,46.25

Prepaid Rent — Account No. 131

DATE	EXPLANATION	P.R.	DEBIT	CREDIT	BALANCE
1993 Dec. 31	Balance				225.00

Office Equipment — Account No. 163

DATE	EXPLANATION	P.R.	DEBIT	CREDIT	BALANCE
1993 Dec. 31	Balance				340.00

SERIAL PROBLEM
Precision Computer Services (Continued)

Accumulated Depreciation, Office Equipment — Account No. 164

DATE	EXPLANATION	P.R.	DEBIT	CREDIT	BALANCE
1993 Dec. 31	Balance				2 1 25

Computer Equipment — Account No. 167

DATE	EXPLANATION	P.R.	DEBIT	CREDIT	BALANCE
1993 Dec. 31	Balance				3 0 0 0 00

Accumulated Depreciation, Computer Equipment — Account No. 168

DATE	EXPLANATION	P.R.	DEBIT	CREDIT	BALANCE
1993 Dec. 31	Balance				2 5 0 00

Accounts Payable — Account No. 201

DATE	EXPLANATION	P.R.	DEBIT	CREDIT	BALANCE
1993 Dec. 31	Balance				8 5 00

Wages Payable — Account No. 210

DATE	EXPLANATION	P.R.	DEBIT	CREDIT	BALANCE
1993 Dec. 31	Balance				2 1 0 00

Unearned Computer Fees — Account No. 233

DATE	EXPLANATION	P.R.	DEBIT	CREDIT	BALANCE
1993 Dec. 31	Balance				4 5 0 00

SERIAL PROBLEM
Precision Computer Services (Continued)

John Conard, Capital — Account No. 301

DATE	EXPLANATION	P.R.	DEBIT	CREDIT	BALANCE
1993 Dec. 31	Balance				8,340 00

John Conard, Withdrawals — Account No. 302

DATE	EXPLANATION	P.R.	DEBIT	CREDIT	BALANCE
1993 Dec. 31	Balance				3,160 00

Computer Services Revenue — Account No. 403

DATE	EXPLANATION	P.R.	DEBIT	CREDIT	BALANCE
1993 Dec. 31	Balance				6,840 00

Depreciation Expense, Office Equipment — Account No. 612

DATE	EXPLANATION	P.R.	DEBIT	CREDIT	BALANCE
1993 Dec. 31	Balance				21 25

Depreciation Expense, Computer Equipment — Account No. 613

DATE	EXPLANATION	P.R.	DEBIT	CREDIT	BALANCE
1993 Dec. 31	Balance				250 00

SERIAL PROBLEM
Precision Computer Services (Continued)

Wages Expense — Account No. 623

DATE	EXPLANATION	P.R.	DEBIT	CREDIT	BALANCE
1993 Dec. 31	Balance				1 680 00

Insurance Expense — Account No. 637

DATE	EXPLANATION	P.R.	DEBIT	CREDIT	BALANCE
1993 Dec. 31	Balance				48 75

Rent Expense — Account No. 640

DATE	EXPLANATION	P.R.	DEBIT	CREDIT	BALANCE
1993 Dec. 31	Balance				675 00

Computer Supplies Expense — Account No. 652

DATE	EXPLANATION	P.R.	DEBIT	CREDIT	BALANCE
1993 Dec. 31	Balance				218 00

Advertising Expense — Account No. 655

DATE	EXPLANATION	P.R.	DEBIT	CREDIT	BALANCE
1993 Dec. 31	Balance				330 00

Working Papers, Chapter 4

SERIAL PROBLEM
Precision Computer Services (Continued)

	Mileage Expense				Account No. 676
DATE	EXPLANATION	P.R.	DEBIT	CREDIT	BALANCE
1993 Dec. 31	Balance				396 00

	Miscellaneous Expenses				Account No. 677
DATE	EXPLANATION	P.R.	DEBIT	CREDIT	BALANCE
1993 Dec. 31	Balance				18 00

	Repairs Expense, Computer				Account No. 684
DATE	EXPLANATION	P.R.	DEBIT	CREDIT	BALANCE
1993 Dec. 31	Balance				101 00

	Telephone Expense				Account No. 688
DATE	EXPLANATION	P.R.	DEBIT	CREDIT	BALANCE
1993 Dec. 31	Balance				343 00

	Utilities Expense				Account No. 690
DATE	EXPLANATION	P.R.	DEBIT	CREDIT	BALANCE
1993 Dec. 31	Balance				147 00

SERIAL PROBLEM
Precision Computer Services (Concluded)

Name _____

	Income Summary				Account No. 901
DATE	EXPLANATION	P.R.	DEBIT	CREDIT	BALANCE

PRECISION COMPUTER SERVICES
Post-Closing Trial Balance
December 31, 1993

CHAPTER 5   EXERCISE 5-1   Name _____

GENERAL JOURNAL   Page 1

DATE	ACCOUNT TITLES AND EXPLANATION	P.R.	DEBIT	CREDIT

EXERCISE 5-2

GENERAL JOURNAL   Page 1

DATE	ACCOUNT TITLES AND EXPLANATION	P.R.	DEBIT	CREDIT

CHAPTER 5   EXERCISE 5-3

GENERAL JOURNAL   Page 1

DATE	ACCOUNT TITLES AND EXPLANATION	P.R.	DEBIT	CREDIT

EXERCISE 5-4

SALES	BEGINNING INVENTORY	PURCHASES	ENDING INVENTORY	COST OF GOODS SOLD	GROSS PROFIT	EXPENSES	NET INCOME OR LOSS
$198,000	$144,000	$126,000	$_____	$171,000	$_____	$90,000	$_____
333,000	117,000	_____	135,000	144,000	_____	99,000	90,000
270,000	90,000	_____	54,000	_____	153,000	81,000	72,000
_____	135,000	198,000	108,000	_____	180,000	72,000	_____
288,000	108,000	171,000	_____	189,000	_____	126,000	_____
90,000	27,000	_____	45,000	54,000	_____	_____	9,000
_____	207,000	396,000	234,000	_____	252,000	_____	90,000
144,000	_____	90,000	63,000	_____	54,000	_____	18,000

Fundamental Accounting Principles, 13/e.

CHAPTER 5   EXERCISE 5-5

The Cottage
Income Statement
For Year Ended December 31, 1993

Revenue from sales:			
Sales			360000 —
Less: Sales Returns + Allowances		2250 —	
Sales discounts		2700 —	4950
Net Sales			355050
Cost of Goods Sold			
Merchandise Inventory, January 1, 1993		64500 —	
Purchases	216000 —		
Less: Purchases returns + allowances 1500			
Purchase discounts 4500	6000 —		
Net Purchases	210000 —		
Add: Transportation-in	1050 —		
Cost of Goods purchased		211050 —	
Cost of Goods available for sell		275550 —	
Less: Inventory December 31, 1994		72000 —	
Cost of Goods Sold			203550 —
Gross Profit from sales			151500 —
Operating expenses:			
Selling expenses		54000 —	
General and Administrative expenses		37500 —	
Total operating expenses			91500 —
Net income			60000 —

CHAPTER 5　　EXERCISE 5-6
Part 1

GENERAL JOURNAL　　　　　　　　　　　　　　Page 1

DATE	ACCOUNT TITLES AND EXPLANATION	P.R.	DEBIT	CREDIT

Part 2

GENERAL LEDGER

Merchandise Inventory　　　　　　　　　　Account No. 119

DATE	EXPLANATION	P.R.	DEBIT	CREDIT	BALANCE

CHAPTER 5   **EXERCISE 5-7**   Name _____

CHAPTER 5   EXERCISE 5-8

Revenue from sales:						
Sales						$540000 —
Less: Sales Returns + Allowances				2700 —		
Sales discounts				5400 —	8100 —	
Net Sales						$531900 —
Cost of Goods Sold						
Beginning Inventory, January 1/1993				$71000 —		
Purchases	324000 —					
Less: Purchase returns + allowances $1800						
Purchase discounts 4500		6300 —				
Net Purchases	317700 —					
Add: Transportation-in		900 —				
Cost of Goods Purchased				318600 —		
Cost of Goods Available for sell				$389600 —		
Less: Ending Inventory Dec. 31/1993				90000 —		
Cost of Goods Sold					299600 —	
Gross Profit from Sales						$232300 —
Operating expenses:						
Selling expenses				81000 —		
General & administrative expenses				63900 —		
Total expenses					144900 —	
Income from operations						$87400 —
Less: Income tax expense						14400 —
Net income						$73000

Balance — beginning of period						$160500 —
Add: net income						73000 —
Total						233500 —
Deduct: dividends declared						30000 —
Balance — end of period						$203500 —

CHAPTER 5 EXERCISE 5-9 Name _____
Part 1

GENERAL JOURNAL   Page 1

DATE	ACCOUNT TITLES AND EXPLANATION	P.R.	DEBIT	CREDIT

Part 2

GENERAL LEDGER

Merchandise Inventory   Account No. 119

DATE	EXPLANATION	P.R.	DEBIT	CREDIT	BALANCE

CHAPTER 5   EXERCISE 5-10

CHAPTER 5 EXERCISE 5-11 Name _____

CROWN, INCORPORATED
Work Sheet
For Year Ended December 31, 1993

ACCOUNT TITLES	UNADJUSTED TRIAL BALANCE		ADJUSTMENTS		INCOME STATEMENT		RETAINED EARNINGS STATEMENT OR BALANCE SHEET	
	DR.	CR.	DR.	CR.	DR.	CR.	DR.	CR.

Working Papers, Chapter 5

CHAPTER 5   **EXERCISE 5-12**

CROWN, INCORPORATED
Work Sheet
For Year Ended December 31, 1993

ACCOUNT TITLES	UNADJUSTED TRIAL BALANCE DR.	CR.	ADJUSTMENTS DR.	CR.	INCOME STATEMENT DR.	CR.	RETAINED EARNINGS STATEMENT OR BALANCE SHEET DR.	CR.

CHAPTER 5 **EXERCISE 5-13** Name _____

GENERAL JOURNAL
Page 1

DATE	ACCOUNT TITLES AND EXPLANATION	P.R.	DEBIT	CREDIT

CHAPTER 5 EXERCISE 5-14

MARTIN SALES
Work Sheet
For Year Ended December 31, 1993

ACCOUNT TITLES	UNADJUSTED TRIAL BALANCE DR.	UNADJUSTED TRIAL BALANCE CR.	ADJUSTMENTS DR.	ADJUSTMENTS CR.	INCOME STATEMENT DR.	INCOME STATEMENT CR.	STATEMENT OF CHANGES IN OWNER'S EQUITY OR BALANCE SHEET DR.	STATEMENT OF CHANGES IN OWNER'S EQUITY OR BALANCE SHEET CR.
Cash	$12 —						12 —	
A/R	16 —						16 —	
Merchandise Inventory	24 —				24 —	32 —	32 —	
Store Supplies	14 —			a) 7 —			7 —	
A/P		28 —						28 —
Salaries payable				b) 5 —				5 —
Jim Martin, capital		39 —						9 —
" w/drawals	9 —						9 —	
Sales		93 —				93 —		
Sales Returns & Allowance	8 —				8 —			
Purchase	37 —				37 —			
Purchases discounts		6 —				6 —		
Transportation-in	7 —				7 —			
Salaries expense	28 —		b) 5 —		33 —			
Rent expense	11 —				4 —			
Store Supplies expense			a) 7 —		7 —			
Total	166 —	166 —	12 —	12 —	127 —	131 —	76 —	72 —
					4 —			4 —
					131 —	131 —	76 —	76 —

CHAPTER 5 EXERCISE 5-15

MARTIN SALES
Work Sheet
For Year Ended December 31, 1993

ACCOUNT TITLES	UNADJUSTED TRIAL BALANCE		ADJUSTMENTS		INCOME STATEMENT		STATEMENT OF CHANGES IN OWNER'S EQUITY OR BALANCE SHEET	
	DR.	CR.	DR.	CR.	DR.	CR.	DR.	CR.

Working Papers, Chapter 5

CHAPTER 5 **EXERCISE 5-16**

GENERAL JOURNAL Page 1

DATE	ACCOUNT TITLES AND EXPLANATION	P.R.	DEBIT	CREDIT

CHAPTER 5 PROBLEM 5-1 or 5-1A

GENERAL JOURNAL Page 1

DATE	ACCOUNT TITLES AND EXPLANATION	P.R.	DEBIT	CREDIT
2	Purchases		4700	
	A.P			4700
3	Office Equip		10000	
	A.P			10000
3	A.R		2900	
	Sales			2900
4	Transportation-In		225	
	Cash			225
8	Cash		470	
	Sales			470
10	Purchases		2600	
	A.P			2600
12	A.P		400	
	Purchases Returns & All.			400
19	A.R		2460	
	Sales			2460
22	Sales R.+A		335	
	A.R.			335
23	Office Supplies		295	
	A.P			295
24	A.P		70	
	Office Supplies			70
25	A.P (2600-400)		2200	
	Purchases Discounts (2200 × .02)			44
	Cash			2156
29	Cash S.		2871	
	Sales Disc. (2900 × .01)		29	
	A.R			2900

CHAPTER 5   PROBLEM 5-1 or 5-1A (Concluded)

Page 2

DATE	ACCOUNT TITLES AND EXPLANATION	P.R.	DEBIT	CREDIT
29	Cash		2410 80	
	Sales disc.		49 20	
	Sales			2460 —
Oct. 1	Cash		4700 —	
	A.P.			4700 —

CHAPTER 5   PROBLEM 5-2 or 5-2A
Part 1

Name _____

Income Statement
4 Year Ended.

Sales				396612 —
Sales Returns & Allowances			2364 —	
Net Sales				394248 —
Beginning Inventory, Jan. 1/93			40518 —	
Purchases	260118 —			
Purchases Returns + Allow. 936				
Purchases Discounts 3906	4842 —			
Net Purchases	255276 —			
Add: Transportation In	1686 —			
Cost of Goods Purchased			256962 —	
Cost of Goods Available for sale			297480 —	
Less: Ending Inventory, Dec. 31/93			42948 —	
Cost of Goods Sold				254532 —
Gross Profit from Sales				139716 —
OPERATING EXPENSES:				
Selling Expenses:				
Amort. Exp. Store Equip.	3810 —			
Sales Salaries Exp.	39312 —			
Rent Exp, Selling space	19440 —			
Store Supplies Exp.	990 —			
Advertising Exp.	1422 —			
Total Selling Exp.			64974 —	
General + Admin. Exp.				
Amort. Exp. Office Equip.	954 —			
Office Salaries Exp.	19170 —			
Insurance Exp.	2592 —			
Rent Exp, Office space	2160 —			
Office Supplies Exp.	390 —			
Telephone Exp.	1026 —			
Total Gen. + Admin. Expense			26292 —	
Total Operating Expense				91266 —
Income from operations				48450 —
Less: Income tax				6786 —
Net Income				41664 —

CHAPTER 5   PROBLEM 5-2 or 5-2A (Continued)
Part 2

Hodgeson Sales Inc's
Retained Earnings
For Year ended Dec. 31/93

Balance beginning inventory			120,000
Add net income			41,684
Total			161,684
Deduct cash dividends declared			30,000
Balance end of period			131,684

Parts 3 and 4

GENERAL JOURNAL   Page 1

DATE	ACCOUNT TITLES AND EXPLANATION	P.R.	DEBIT	CREDIT

222   *Fundamental Accounting Principles, 13/e.*

CHAPTER 5   PROBLEM 5-2 or 5-2A (Continued)   Name _____

Page 2

DATE	ACCOUNT TITLES AND EXPLANATION	P.R.	DEBIT	CREDIT

Part 4

GENERAL LEDGER

Merchandise Inventory   Account No. 119

DATE	EXPLANATION	P.R.	DEBIT	CREDIT	BALANCE

Working Papers, Chapter 5

CHAPTER 5 PROBLEM 5-2 or 5-2A (Concluded)
Part 5

CHAPTER 5 PROBLEM 5-3 or 5-3A Name _____

(The work sheet for this problem is in the back of this booklet.)

Parts 2 and 3

GENERAL JOURNAL Page 1

DATE	ACCOUNT TITLES AND EXPLANATION	P.R.	DEBIT	CREDIT

Working Papers, Chapter 5

225

CHAPTER 5   PROBLEM 5-3 or 5-3A (Concluded)

Page 2

DATE	ACCOUNT TITLES AND EXPLANATION	P.R.	DEBIT	CREDIT

Part 3

GENERAL LEDGER

Merchandise Inventory — Account No. 119

DATE	EXPLANATION	P.R.	DEBIT	CREDIT	BALANCE

CHAPTER 5 PROBLEM 5-4 or 5-4A Name _____

(The work sheet for this problem is in the back of this booklet.)

Parts 2 and 3

GENERAL JOURNAL Page 1

DATE	ACCOUNT TITLES AND EXPLANATION	P.R.	DEBIT	CREDIT

Working Papers, Chapter 5

CHAPTER 5   PROBLEM 5-4 or 5-4A (Concluded)

Page 2

DATE	ACCOUNT TITLES AND EXPLANATION	P.R.	DEBIT	CREDIT

Part 3

GENERAL LEDGER

Merchandise Inventory   Account No. 119

DATE	EXPLANATION	P.R.	DEBIT	CREDIT	BALANCE

CHAPTER 5   PROBLEM 5-5 or 5-5A   Name _____
(The work sheet for this problem is in the back of this booklet.)
Part 2

CHAPTER 5　　PROBLEM 5-5 or 5-5A (Continued)
Part 3

CHAPTER 5　PROBLEM 5-5 or 5-5A (Continued)
Part 4

Name _____

GENERAL JOURNAL　　　　　Page 1

DATE	ACCOUNT TITLES AND EXPLANATION	P.R.	DEBIT	CREDIT

CHAPTER 5   PROBLEM 5-5 or 5-5A (Concluded)

Page 2

DATE	ACCOUNT TITLES AND EXPLANATION	P.R.	DEBIT	CREDIT

Part 5

CHAPTER 5   **PROBLEM 5-6 or 5-6A**   Name _____

(The work sheet for this problem is in the back of this booklet.)

Part 2

CHAPTER 5   PROBLEM 5-6 or 5-6A (Continued)
Part 3

Part 4

	GENERAL JOURNAL			Page 1
DATE	ACCOUNT TITLES AND EXPLANATION	P.R.	DEBIT	CREDIT

CHAPTER 5   PROBLEM 5-6 or 5-6A (Continued)   Name _____

Page 2

DATE	ACCOUNT TITLES AND EXPLANATION	P.R.	DEBIT	CREDIT

CHAPTER 5 PROBLEM 5-6 or 5-6A (Concluded)

Page 3

DATE	ACCOUNT TITLES AND EXPLANATION	P.R.	DEBIT	CREDIT

Part 5

CHAPTER 5 PROBLEM 5-7 or 5-7A Name _____
(The work sheet for this problem is in the back of this booklet.)
Part 2

CHAPTER 5   PROBLEM 5-7 or 5-7A (Continued)

Part 3

Part 4

CHAPTER 5 PROBLEM 5-7 or 5-7A (Continued) Name _____
Part 5

GENERAL JOURNAL
Page 1

DATE	ACCOUNT TITLES AND EXPLANATION	P.R.	DEBIT	CREDIT

CHAPTER 5   PROBLEM 5-7 or 5-7A (Concluded)

Page 2

DATE	ACCOUNT TITLES AND EXPLANATION	P.R.	DEBIT	CREDIT

CHAPTER 5   **PROBLEM 5-8 or 5-8A**   Name _____

CHAPTER 5 PROBLEM 5-8 or 5-8A (Concluded)

CHAPTER 5   PROBLEM 5-9 or 5-9A   Name _____

CHAPTER 5   **PROBLEM 5-9 or 5-9A (Concluded)**

SERIAL PROBLEM
Precision Computer Services
(The work sheet for this problem is in the back of this booklet.)

GENERAL JOURNAL — Page 9

DATE	ACCOUNT TITLES AND EXPLANATION	P.R.	DEBIT	CREDIT

SERIAL PROBLEM
Precision Computer Services (Continued)

Page 10

DATE	ACCOUNT TITLES AND EXPLANATION	P.R.	DEBIT	CREDIT

SERIAL PROBLEM
Precision Computer Services (Continued)

Page 11

DATE	ACCOUNT TITLES AND EXPLANATION	P.R.	DEBIT	CREDIT

SERIAL PROBLEM
Precision Computer Services (Continued)

Page 12

DATE	ACCOUNT TITLES AND EXPLANATION	P.R.	DEBIT	CREDIT

SERIAL PROBLEM
Precision Computer Services (Continued)

Name _____

Page 13

DATE	ACCOUNT TITLES AND EXPLANATION	P.R.	DEBIT	CREDIT

SERIAL PROBLEM
Precision Computer Services (Continued)

Page 14

DATE	ACCOUNT TITLES AND EXPLANATION	P.R.	DEBIT	CREDIT

SERIAL PROBLEM
Precision Computer Services (Continued)

GENERAL LEDGER

Cash Account   Account No. 101

DATE	EXPLANATION	P.R.	DEBIT	CREDIT	BALANCE
1993 Dec. 31	Balance				4,410.00

Working Papers, Chapter 5

SERIAL PROBLEM
Precision Computer Services (Continued)

Account Receivable—AB Company   Account No. 1060

DATE	EXPLANATION	P.R.	DEBIT	CREDIT	BALANCE

Account Receivable—Ball Company   Account No. 1061

DATE	EXPLANATION	P.R.	DEBIT	CREDIT	BALANCE

Account Receivable—Call Company   Account No. 1062

DATE	EXPLANATION	P.R.	DEBIT	CREDIT	BALANCE
1993 Dec. 31	Balance				225 00

Account Receivable—Dog Enterprise   Account No. 1063

DATE	EXPLANATION	P.R.	DEBIT	CREDIT	BALANCE

Account Receivable—Ear Hearing   Account No. 1064

DATE	EXPLANATION	P.R.	DEBIT	CREDIT	BALANCE

SERIAL PROBLEM
Precision Computer Services (Continued)

Name _____

Account Receivable—Farm Research   Account No. 1065

DATE	EXPLANATION	P.R.	DEBIT	CREDIT	BALANCE
1993 Dec. 31	Balance				445 00

Account Receivable—Goodall Limited   Account No. 1066

DATE	EXPLANATION	P.R.	DEBIT	CREDIT	BALANCE

Account Receivable—Iceman, Inc.   Account No. 1067

DATE	EXPLANATION	P.R.	DEBIT	CREDIT	BALANCE

Account Receivable—Jackets and More   Account No. 1068

DATE	EXPLANATION	P.R.	DEBIT	CREDIT	BALANCE

Computer Supplies   Account No. 126

DATE	EXPLANATION	P.R.	DEBIT	CREDIT	BALANCE
1993 Dec. 31	Balance				17 00

SERIAL PROBLEM
Precision Computer Services (Continued)

Prepaid Insurance — Account No. 128

DATE	EXPLANATION	P.R.	DEBIT	CREDIT	BALANCE
1993 Dec. 31	Balance				146 25

Prepaid Rent — Account No. 131

DATE	EXPLANATION	P.R.	DEBIT	CREDIT	BALANCE
1993 Dec. 31	Balance				225 00

Office Equipment — Account No. 163

DATE	EXPLANATION	P.R.	DEBIT	CREDIT	BALANCE
1993 Dec. 31	Balance				340 00

Accumulated Depreciation, Office Equipment — Account No. 164

DATE	EXPLANATION	P.R.	DEBIT	CREDIT	BALANCE
1993 Dec. 31	Balance				21 25

Computer Equipment — Account No. 167

DATE	EXPLANATION	P.R.	DEBIT	CREDIT	BALANCE
1993 Dec. 31	Balance				3000 00

SERIAL PROBLEM
Precision Computer Services (Continued)

Name _____

Accumulated Depreciation, Computer Equipment — Account No. 168

DATE	EXPLANATION	P.R.	DEBIT	CREDIT	BALANCE
1993 Dec. 31	Balance				250 00

Accounts Payable — Account No. 201

DATE	EXPLANATION	P.R.	DEBIT	CREDIT	BALANCE
1993 Dec. 31	Balance				85 00

Wages Payable — Account No. 210

DATE	EXPLANATION	P.R.	DEBIT	CREDIT	BALANCE
1993 Dec. 31	Balance				210 00

SERIAL PROBLEM
Precision Computer Services (Continued)

Unearned Computer Fees — Account No. 233

DATE	EXPLANATION	P.R.	DEBIT	CREDIT	BALANCE
1993 Dec. 31	Balance				450 00

John Conard, Capital — Account No. 301

DATE	EXPLANATION	P.R.	DEBIT	CREDIT	BALANCE
1993 Dec. 31	Balance				7 792 00

John Conard, Withdrawals — Account No. 302

DATE	EXPLANATION	P.R.	DEBIT	CREDIT	BALANCE

Computer Services Revenue — Account No. 403

DATE	EXPLANATION	P.R.	DEBIT	CREDIT	BALANCE

SERIAL PROBLEM
Precision Computer Services (Continued)

Name _____

Sales   Account No. 413

DATE	EXPLANATION	P.R.	DEBIT	CREDIT	BALANCE

Sales Returns and Allowances   Account No. 414

DATE	EXPLANATION	P.R.	DEBIT	CREDIT	BALANCE

Sales Discounts   Account No. 415

DATE	EXPLANATION	P.R.	DEBIT	CREDIT	BALANCE

Purchases   Account No. 505

DATE	EXPLANATION	P.R.	DEBIT	CREDIT	BALANCE

Purchases Returns and Allowances   Account No. 506

DATE	EXPLANATION	P.R.	DEBIT	CREDIT	BALANCE

Purchases Discounts   Account No. 507

DATE	EXPLANATION	P.R.	DEBIT	CREDIT	BALANCE

SERIAL PROBLEM
Precision Computer Services (Continued)

Transportation-In — Account No. 508

DATE	EXPLANATION	P.R.	DEBIT	CREDIT	BALANCE

Depreciation Expense, Office Equipment — Account No. 612

DATE	EXPLANATION	P.R.	DEBIT	CREDIT	BALANCE

Depreciation Expense, Computer Equipment — Account No. 613

DATE	EXPLANATION	P.R.	DEBIT	CREDIT	BALANCE

Wages Expense — Account No. 623

DATE	EXPLANATION	P.R.	DEBIT	CREDIT	BALANCE

Insurance Expense — Account No. 637

DATE	EXPLANATION	P.R.	DEBIT	CREDIT	BALANCE

Rent Expense — Account No. 640

DATE	EXPLANATION	P.R.	DEBIT	CREDIT	BALANCE

SERIAL PROBLEM
Precision Computer Services (Continued)

Name _____

Computer Supplies Expense — Account No. 652

DATE	EXPLANATION	P.R.	DEBIT	CREDIT	BALANCE

Advertising Expense — Account No. 655

DATE	EXPLANATION	P.R.	DEBIT	CREDIT	BALANCE

Mileage Expense — Account No. 676

DATE	EXPLANATION	P.R.	DEBIT	CREDIT	BALANCE

Miscellaneous Expenses — Account No. 677

DATE	EXPLANATION	P.R.	DEBIT	CREDIT	BALANCE

Repairs Expense, Computer — Account No. 684

DATE	EXPLANATION	P.R.	DEBIT	CREDIT	BALANCE

Telephone Expense — Account No. 688

DATE	EXPLANATION	P.R.	DEBIT	CREDIT	BALANCE

SERIAL PROBLEM
Precision Computer Services (Continued)

	Utilities Expense				Account No. 690
DATE	EXPLANATION	P.R.	DEBIT	CREDIT	BALANCE

	Income Summary				Account No. 901
DATE	EXPLANATION	P.R.	DEBIT	CREDIT	BALANCE

SERIAL PROBLEM
Precision Computer Services (Continued)

PRECISION COMPUTER SERVICES
Income Statement
For Quarter Ended March 31, 1994

SERIAL PROBLEM
Precision Computer Services (Concluded)

PRECISION COMPUTER SERVICES
Statement of Changes in Owner's Equity
For Quarter Ended March 31, 1994

PRECISION COMPUTER SERVICES
Balance Sheet
March 31, 1994

CHAPTER 6   EXERCISE 6-1

(a) Purchase Journal
General Journal
Purchase Journal
Sales Cash Receipts Journal
Sales Journal
Sales Journal
General Journal
General Journal
Sales Purchases Journal
General Journal
Cash Disbursements

SALES JOURNAL

Page 2

DATE	ACCOUNT DEBITED	INVOICE NUMBER	P.R.	AMOUNT

EXERCISE 6-2

Working Papers, Chapter 6   263

CHAPTER 6   EXERCISE 6-3

CASH RECEIPTS JOURNAL   Page 3

DATE	ACCOUNT CREDITED	EXPLANATION	P.R.	OTHER ACCOUNTS CREDIT	ACCOUNTS RECEIVABLE CREDIT	SALES CREDIT	SALES DISCOUNTS DEBIT	CASH DEBIT
Oct. 2	F. Ray, Capital	investment		7000 —				7000 —
Oct. 14	Notes Payable	note to bank		1500 —				1500 —
Oct. 15	Sales	cash sale				240 —		240 —
Oct. 28	D. Parker	invoice, 10/11			3750 —		75 —	3675 —

EXERCISE 6-4

PURCHASES JOURNAL   Page 2

DATE	ACCOUNT	DATE OF INVOICE	TERMS	P.R.	PURCHASES DEBIT	OFFICE SUPPLIES DEBIT	OTHER ACCOUNTS DEBIT	ACCOUNTS PAYABLE CREDIT
May 4	Isle Company	4/5	n/30		4400 —			4400 —
May 17	Store Supplies / D. Company	12/5	n/30			90 —	175 —	265 —

EXERCISE 6-5

CASH DISBURSEMENTS JOURNAL   Page 3

DATE	CH. NO.	PAYEE	ACCOUNT DEBITED	P.R.	OTHER ACCOUNTS DEBIT	ACCOUNTS PAYABLE DEBIT	PURCHASES DISCOUNTS CREDIT	CASH CREDIT
Aug. 7	57	T Company	Store Supplies		88 —			88 —
Aug. 18	58	State Bank	Note Payable		270 —			270 —
Aug. 19	59	B+B Company	Accounts Payable			3300 —	66 —	3234 —
Aug. 31	60	Z+P Company	Accounts Payable			1100 —		1100 —
					358 —	4400 —	66 —	4692 —

Fundamental Accounting Principles, 13/e.

CHAPTER 6   EXERCISE 6-6   Name _____

GENERAL JOURNAL   Page 1

DATE	ACCOUNT TITLES AND EXPLANATION	P.R.	DEBIT	CREDIT

EXERCISE 6-7

CHAPTER 6   EXERCISE 6-8
Part 1

ACCOUNTS RECEIVABLE LEDGER

Tomas Cantu		Sheila Lee		Barbara Lyon	
June 18 1280		June 3 845		June 12 630	June 15 140
" 23 460				490	
1740					

Part 2

GENERAL LEDGER

Accounts Receivable		Sales		Sales Returns and Allowances	
June 30 3215	June 15 140		June 30 3215	June 14 140	
3075					

Part 3

Abilene Company
Subsidiary Accounts Receivable
June 30, 1994

Sheila Lee	845 —
Barbara Lyon	490 —
Tomas Cantu	1740 —
Total accts. rec.	3075 —

Accounts Receivable	
Total Debit	3215 —
Credit for return	(140)
Balance as of June 30, 19—	3075 —

CHAPTER 6 EXERCISE 6-9 Name _____
Part 1

ACCOUNTS RECEIVABLE LEDGER

Milton Gibbs

Teresa Katz

Sam Smith

Arnold Swartz

Part 2

GENERAL JOURNAL   Page 1

DATE	ACCOUNT TITLES AND EXPLANATION	P.R.	DEBIT	CREDIT

Part 3

GENERAL LEDGER

Accounts Receivable

Sales

Part 4

CHAPTER 6   EXERCISE 6-10

GENERAL LEDGER

| Cash | Accounts Payable | Sales Discounts |

| Accounts Receivable | Notes Payable | Purchases |

| Prepaid Insurance | Sales | Purchases Returns and Allowances |

| Store Equipment | Sales Returns and Allowances | Purchases Discounts |

ACCOUNTS RECEIVABLE LEDGER

| Customer A | Customer B | Customer C |

ACCOUNTS PAYABLE LEDGER

| Company One | Company Two | Company Three |

CHAPTER 6   EXERCISE 6-11

CHAPTER 6 PROBLEM 6-1 or 6-1A

Name _____

SALES JOURNAL

Page 3

DATE	ACCOUNT DEBITED	INVOICE NUMBER	P.R.	AMOUNT
Nov. 3	Accounts Receivable – Frank Mendoza	530		1 600 —
Nov. 5	Accounts Receivable – Janet Dalton	531		4 850 —
Nov. 11	Accounts Receivable – Cynthia Montgomery	532		7 600 —
Nov. 15	Accounts Receivable – Frank Mendoza	533		3 250 —
Nov. 27	Accounts Receivable – Janet Dalton	534		2 460 —
Nov. 28	Accounts Receivable – Cynthia Montgomery	535		4 620 —

CASH RECEIPTS JOURNAL

Page 3

DATE	ACCOUNT CREDITED	EXPLANATION	P.R.	OTHER ACCOUNTS CREDIT	ACCOUNTS RECEIVABLE CREDIT	SALES CREDIT	SALES DISCOUNTS DEBIT	CASH DEBIT
Nov. 13	Accounts Receivable				1 110 —			1 110 —
Nov. 15	"				40 670 —			40 670 —
Nov. 15	"				4 850 —			4 850 —
Nov. 18	Notes Payable			32 000 —				32 000 —
Nov. 21	Accounts Receivable				7 600 —			7 600 —
Nov. 25	"				3 250 —			3 250 —
Nov. 30	Notes Payable			56 780 —				56 780 —

Working Papers, Chapter 6

CHAPTER 6   PROBLEM 6-1 or 6-1A (Continued)

GENERAL LEDGER

Cash — Account No. 101

DATE	EXPLANATION	P.R.	DEBIT	CREDIT	BALANCE
Nov. 30			146 260 —		146 260 —

Accounts Receivable — Account No. 106

DATE	EXPLANATION	P.R.	DEBIT	CREDIT	BALANCE
Nov. 30				57 480 —	57 480 —

Notes Payable — Account No. 251

DATE	EXPLANATION	P.R.	DEBIT	CREDIT	BALANCE
Nov. 30				88 780 —	88 780 —

Sales — Account No. 413

DATE	EXPLANATION	P.R.	DEBIT	CREDIT	BALANCE

Sales Discounts — Account No. 415

DATE	EXPLANATION	P.R.	DEBIT	CREDIT	BALANCE

Fundamental Accounting Principles, 13/e.

CHAPTER 6   PROBLEM 6-1 or 6-1A (Continued)   Name _____

ACCOUNTS RECEIVABLE LEDGER

NAME   Janet Dalton
ADDRESS   1008 High Street

DATE	EXPLANATION	P.R.	DEBIT	CREDIT	BALANCE
Nov. 5				4 850 —	4 850 —
Nov. 27				2 460 —	7 310 —

NAME   Frank Mendoza
ADDRESS   1217 Adler Street

DATE	EXPLANATION	P.R.	DEBIT	CREDIT	BALANCE
Nov. 3				1 600 —	1 600 —
Nov. 15				3 250 —	4 850 —

NAME   Cynthia Montgomery
ADDRESS   507 East 10th Street

DATE	EXPLANATION	P.R.	DEBIT	CREDIT	BALANCE
Nov. 11				7 600 —	7 600 —
Nov. 28				4 620 —	12 220 —

Working Papers, Chapter 6

CHAPTER 6   PROBLEM 6-1 or 6-1A (Concluded)

CHAPTER 6 PROBLEM 6-2 or 6-2A Name _____

PURCHASES JOURNAL — Page 3

DATE	ACCOUNT	DATE OF INVOICE	TERMS	P.R.	PURCHASES DEBIT	OTHER ACCOUNTS DEBIT	ACCOUNTS PAYABLE CREDIT

CASH DISBURSEMENTS JOURNAL — Page 3

DATE	CH. NO.	PAYEE	ACCOUNT DEBITED	P.R.	OTHER ACCOUNTS DEBIT	ACCOUNTS PAYABLE DEBIT	PURCHASES DISCOUNTS CREDIT	CASH CREDIT

CHAPTER 6   PROBLEM 6-2 or 6-2A (Continued)

GENERAL JOURNAL   Page 3

DATE	ACCOUNT TITLES AND EXPLANATION	P.R.	DEBIT	CREDIT

GENERAL LEDGER

Cash   Account No. 101

DATE	EXPLANATION	P.R.	DEBIT	CREDIT	BALANCE

Office Supplies   Account No. 124

DATE	EXPLANATION	P.R.	DEBIT	CREDIT	BALANCE

Store Supplies   Account No. 125

DATE	EXPLANATION	P.R.	DEBIT	CREDIT	BALANCE

Store Equipment   Account No. 165

DATE	EXPLANATION	P.R.	DEBIT	CREDIT	BALANCE

CHAPTER 6   PROBLEM 6-2 or 6-2A (Continued)   Name _____

Accounts Payable — Account No. 201

DATE	EXPLANATION	P.R.	DEBIT	CREDIT	BALANCE

Long-Term Notes Payable — Account No. 251

DATE	EXPLANATION	P.R.	DEBIT	CREDIT	BALANCE

Purchases — Account No. 505

DATE	EXPLANATION	P.R.	DEBIT	CREDIT	BALANCE

Purchases Returns and Allowances — Account No. 506

DATE	EXPLANATION	P.R.	DEBIT	CREDIT	BALANCE

Purchases Discounts — Account No. 507

DATE	EXPLANATION	P.R.	DEBIT	CREDIT	BALANCE

Sales Salaries Expense — Account No. 621

DATE	EXPLANATION	P.R.	DEBIT	CREDIT	BALANCE

Working Papers, Chapter 6

CHAPTER 6 PROBLEM 6-2 or 6-2A (Continued)

	Advertising Expense				Account No. 655
DATE	EXPLANATION	P.R.	DEBIT	CREDIT	BALANCE

ACCOUNTS PAYABLE LEDGER

NAME   Century Company
ADDRESS   Cranston, Illinois

DATE	EXPLANATION	P.R.	DEBIT	CREDIT	BALANCE

NAME   Fiore Company
ADDRESS   Derby, Ohio

DATE	EXPLANATION	P.R.	DEBIT	CREDIT	BALANCE

NAME   Kramer Company
ADDRESS   Gosport, Indiana

DATE	EXPLANATION	P.R.	DEBIT	CREDIT	BALANCE

NAME   Weisman Company
ADDRESS   32nd and Maple

DATE	EXPLANATION	P.R.	DEBIT	CREDIT	BALANCE

CHAPTER 6   PROBLEM 6-2 or 6-2A (Concluded)   Name _____

CHAPTER 6   PROBLEM 6-3 or 6-3A   Name _____

SALES JOURNAL

Page 3

DATE		ACCOUNT DEBITED	INVOICE NUMBER	P.R.	AMOUNT
Dec.	6	Fred Bidler	303	√	3 6 4 5 00
	12	Katherine Hoffer	304	√	4 0 5 0 00
	15	Kevin Oliver	305	√	3 4 4 5 00

PURCHASES JOURNAL

Page 2

DATE		ACCOUNT	DATE OF INVOICE	TERMS	P.R.	PURCHASES DEBIT	OFFICE SUPPLIES DEBIT	OTHER ACCOUNTS DEBIT	ACCOUNTS PAYABLE CREDIT
Dec.	2	Walker Company	12/ 2	2/10, n/60		3 6 0 0 00			3 6 0 0 00
	5	Southwest Supply Co.	12/ 3	n/10 EOM		1 3 5 0 00			1 3 5 0 00
	15	Walker Company	12/15	2/10, n/60		4 4 3 5 00			4 4 3 5 00
	15	Starbrite Company	12/15	2/10, n/60		2 9 5 0 00			2 9 5 0 00

Working Papers, Chapter 6

CHAPTER 6 PROBLEM 6-3 or 6-3A (Continued)

CASH RECEIPTS JOURNAL

Page 3

DATE	ACCOUNT CREDITED	EXPLANATION	P.R.	OTHER ACCOUNTS CREDIT	ACCOUNTS RECEIVABLE CREDIT	SALES CREDIT	SALES DISCOUNTS DEBIT	CASH DEBIT
Dec. 2	Maria Perez	Invoice 11/23	√		4750 00		95 00	4655 00
15	Sales	Cash sales	√			43155 00		43155 00
15	Fred Bidler	Invoice 12/6	√		2700 00		54 00	2646 00

CASH DISBURSEMENTS JOURNAL

Page 4

DATE	CH. NO.	PAYEE	ACCOUNT DEBITED	P.R.	OTHER ACCOUNTS DEBIT	ACCOUNTS PAYABLE DEBIT	PURCHASES DISCOUNTS CREDIT	CASH CREDIT
Dec. 2	539	Property Management Co.	Rent Expense	640	2500 00			2500 00
6	540	Eclat Company	Eclat Company	√		4250 00	85 00	4165 00
12	541	Walker Company	Walker Company	√		3600 00	72 00	3528 00
15	542	Mark Arlos	Sales Salaries Expense	621	1800 00			1800 00

CHAPTER 6 PROBLEM 6-3 or 6-3A (Continued)   Name _____

GENERAL JOURNAL Page 2

DATE	ACCOUNT TITLES AND EXPLANATION	P.R.	DEBIT	CREDIT
Dec. 4	Accounts Payable—Eclat Company	201/√	515 00	
	Purchases Returns and Allowances	506		515 00
9	Sales Returns and Allowances	414	945 00	
	Accounts Receivable—Fred Bidler	106/√		945 00

ACCOUNTS RECEIVABLE LEDGER

NAME   Fred Bidler
ADDRESS   4012 West Avenue

DATE	EXPLANATION	P.R.	DEBIT	CREDIT	BALANCE
Dec. 6		S3	3645 00		3645 00
9		G2		945 00	2700 00
15		R3		2700 00	-0-

NAME   Katherine Hoffer
ADDRESS   3434 West 18th Street

DATE	EXPLANATION	P.R.	DEBIT	CREDIT	BALANCE
Dec. 12		S3	4050 00		4050 00

Working Papers, Chapter 6   283

CHAPTER 6 PROBLEM 6–3 or 6–3A (Continued)

NAME Kevin Oliver
ADDRESS 1412 West 24th Street

DATE	EXPLANATION	P.R.	DEBIT	CREDIT	BALANCE
Dec. 15		S3	3445 00		3445 00

NAME Maria Perez
ADDRESS 4314 East Oak Avenue

DATE	EXPLANATION	P.R.	DEBIT	CREDIT	BALANCE
Nov. 23		S2	4750 00		4750 00
Dec. 2		R3		4750 00	-0-

ACCOUNTS PAYABLE LEDGER

NAME Eclat Company
ADDRESS 1010 West 10th Street

DATE	EXPLANATION	P.R.	DEBIT	CREDIT	BALANCE
Nov. 28		P1		4765 00	4765 00
Dec. 4		G2	515 00		4250 00
6		D4	4250 00		-0-

NAME Southwest Supply Company
ADDRESS 711 East 15th Street

DATE	EXPLANATION	P.R.	DEBIT	CREDIT	BALANCE
Dec. 5		P2		1350 00	1350 00

NAME Starbrite Company
ADDRESS 15th and Oak

DATE	EXPLANATION	P.R.	DEBIT	CREDIT	BALANCE
Dec. 15		P2		2950 00	2950 00

CHAPTER 6   PROBLEM 6-3 or 6-3A (Continued)   Name _____

NAME   Walker Company
ADDRESS   818 West Live Oak

DATE	EXPLANATION	P.R.	DEBIT	CREDIT	BALANCE
Dec. 2		P2		3 600 00	3 600 00
12		D4	3 600 00		- 0 -
15		P2		4 435 00	4 435 00

GENERAL LEDGER

Cash   Account No. 101

DATE	EXPLANATION	P.R.	DEBIT	CREDIT	BALANCE
Nov. 30	Balance	√			5 895 00

Accounts Receivable   Account No. 106

DATE	EXPLANATION	P.R.	DEBIT	CREDIT	BALANCE
Nov. 30	Balance	√			4 750 00
Dec. 9		G2		945 00	3 805 00

Merchandise Inventory   Account No. 119

DATE	EXPLANATION	P.R.	DEBIT	CREDIT	BALANCE
Nov. 30	Balance	√			74 420 00

Office Supplies   Account No. 124

DATE	EXPLANATION	P.R.	DEBIT	CREDIT	BALANCE
Nov. 30	Balance	√			675 00

CHAPTER 6 PROBLEM 6-3 or 6-3A (Continued)

Store Supplies — Account No. 125

DATE	EXPLANATION	P.R.	DEBIT	CREDIT	BALANCE
Nov. 30	Balance	√			385 00

Store Equipment — Account No. 165

DATE	EXPLANATION	P.R.	DEBIT	CREDIT	BALANCE
Nov. 30	Balance	√			46,810 00

Accumulated Depreciation, Store Equipment — Account No. 166

DATE	EXPLANATION	P.R.	DEBIT	CREDIT	BALANCE
Nov. 30	Balance	√			10,170 00

Accounts Payable — Account No. 201

DATE	EXPLANATION	P.R.	DEBIT	CREDIT	BALANCE
Nov. 30	Balance	√			4,765 00
Dec. 4		G2	515 00		4,250 00

Carol Morgan, Capital — Account No. 301

DATE	EXPLANATION	P.R.	DEBIT	CREDIT	BALANCE
Nov. 30	Balance	√			11,800 00

Carol Morgan, Withdrawals — Account No. 302

DATE	EXPLANATION	P.R.	DEBIT	CREDIT	BALANCE

CHAPTER 6 PROBLEM 6-3 or 6-3A (Continued) Name _____

Sales — Account No. 413

DATE	EXPLANATION	P.R.	DEBIT	CREDIT	BALANCE

Sales Returns and Allowances — Account No. 414

DATE	EXPLANATION	P.R.	DEBIT	CREDIT	BALANCE
Dec. 9		G2	945 00		945 00

Sales Discounts — Account No. 415

DATE	EXPLANATION	P.R.	DEBIT	CREDIT	BALANCE

Purchases — Account No. 505

DATE	EXPLANATION	P.R.	DEBIT	CREDIT	BALANCE

Purchases Returns and Allowances — Account No. 506

DATE	EXPLANATION	P.R.	DEBIT	CREDIT	BALANCE
Dec. 4		G2		515 00	515 00

Purchases Discounts — Account No. 507

DATE	EXPLANATION	P.R.	DEBIT	CREDIT	BALANCE

Sales Salaries Expense — Account No. 621

DATE	EXPLANATION	P.R.	DEBIT	CREDIT	BALANCE
Dec. 15		D4	1 800 00		1 800 00

Working Papers, Chapter 6

CHAPTER 6   PROBLEM 6-3 or 6-3A (Continued)

	Rent Expense				Account No. 640
DATE	EXPLANATION	P.R.	DEBIT	CREDIT	BALANCE
Dec. 2		D4	2 500 00		2 500 00

	Utilities Expense				Account No. 690
DATE	EXPLANATION	P.R.	DEBIT	CREDIT	BALANCE

CHAPTER 6   **PROBLEM 6-3 or 6-3A (Concluded)**   Name _____

CHAPTER 6 PROBLEM 6-4 or 6-4A

SALES JOURNAL

Page 2

DATE	ACCOUNT DEBITED	INVOICE NUMBER	P.R.	AMOUNT

PURCHASES JOURNAL

Page 2

DATE	ACCOUNT	DATE OF INVOICE	TERMS	P.R.	PURCHASES DEBIT	OFFICE SUPPLIES DEBIT	OTHER ACCOUNTS DEBIT	ACCOUNTS PAYABLE CREDIT

CHAPTER 6   PROBLEM 6-4 or 6-4A (Continued)

CASH RECEIPTS JOURNAL   Page 2

DATE	ACCOUNT CREDITED	EXPLANATION	P.R.	OTHER ACCOUNTS CREDIT	ACCOUNTS RECEIVABLE CREDIT	SALES CREDIT	SALES DISCOUNTS DEBIT	CASH DEBIT

CASH DISBURSEMENTS JOURNAL   Page 2

DATE	CH. NO.	PAYEE	ACCOUNT DEBITED	P.R.	OTHER ACCOUNTS DEBIT	ACCOUNTS PAYABLE DEBIT	PURCHASES DISCOUNTS CREDIT	CASH CREDIT

Fundamental Accounting Principles, 13/e.

CHAPTER 6   PROBLEM 6-4 or 6-4A (Continued)   Name _____

GENERAL JOURNAL   Page 2

DATE	ACCOUNT TITLES AND EXPLANATION	P.R.	DEBIT	CREDIT

GENERAL LEDGER

Cash   Account No. 101

DATE	EXPLANATION	P.R.	DEBIT	CREDIT	BALANCE

Accounts Receivable   Account No. 106

DATE	EXPLANATION	P.R.	DEBIT	CREDIT	BALANCE

Office Supplies   Account No. 124

DATE	EXPLANATION	P.R.	DEBIT	CREDIT	BALANCE

Store Supplies   Account No. 125

DATE	EXPLANATION	P.R.	DEBIT	CREDIT	BALANCE

Working Papers, Chapter 6

CHAPTER 6   PROBLEM 6-4 or 6-4A (Continued)

Office Equipment   Account No. 163

DATE	EXPLANATION	P.R.	DEBIT	CREDIT	BALANCE

Accounts Payable   Account No. 201

DATE	EXPLANATION	P.R.	DEBIT	CREDIT	BALANCE

Long-Term Notes Payable   Account No. 251

DATE	EXPLANATION	P.R.	DEBIT	CREDIT	BALANCE

Sales   Account No. 413

DATE	EXPLANATION	P.R.	DEBIT	CREDIT	BALANCE

Sales Discounts   Account No. 415

DATE	EXPLANATION	P.R.	DEBIT	CREDIT	BALANCE

Purchases   Account No. 505

DATE	EXPLANATION	P.R.	DEBIT	CREDIT	BALANCE

CHAPTER 6 PROBLEM 6-4 or 6-4A (Continued) Name _____

Purchases Returns and Allowances — Account No. 506

DATE	EXPLANATION	P.R.	DEBIT	CREDIT	BALANCE

Purchases Discounts — Account No. 507

DATE	EXPLANATION	P.R.	DEBIT	CREDIT	BALANCE

Sales Salaries Expense — Account No. 621

DATE	EXPLANATION	P.R.	DEBIT	CREDIT	BALANCE

ACCOUNTS RECEIVABLE LEDGER

NAME Margo Edwards
ADDRESS 4314 East Oak Avenue

DATE	EXPLANATION	P.R.	DEBIT	CREDIT	BALANCE

NAME John Nelson
ADDRESS 1412 West 24th Street

DATE	EXPLANATION	P.R.	DEBIT	CREDIT	BALANCE

NAME Thomas Zak
ADDRESS 3434 West 18th Street

DATE	EXPLANATION	P.R.	DEBIT	CREDIT	BALANCE

CHAPTER 6   PROBLEM 6-4 or 6-4A (Continued)

ACCOUNTS PAYABLE LEDGER

NAME   Corsair Company
ADDRESS   1212 Ninth Avenue

DATE	EXPLANATION	P.R.	DEBIT	CREDIT	BALANCE

NAME   Farnswood Company
ADDRESS   15th and Oak

DATE	EXPLANATION	P.R.	DEBIT	CREDIT	BALANCE

NAME   McKay Company
ADDRESS   32nd and Maple

DATE	EXPLANATION	P.R.	DEBIT	CREDIT	BALANCE

NAME   Wellsbranch Company
ADDRESS   1412 East Maple Avenue

DATE	EXPLANATION	P.R.	DEBIT	CREDIT	BALANCE

Fundamental Accounting Principles, 13/e.

CHAPTER 6 PROBLEM 6-4 or 6-4A (Concluded)   Name _____

CHAPTER 6　　PROBLEM 6–5 or 6–5A　　　　　　　　　　Name _____

SALES JOURNAL — Page 3

DATE	ACCOUNT DEBITED	INVOICE NUMBER	P.R.	AMOUNT

PURCHASES JOURNAL — Page 3

DATE	ACCOUNT	DATE OF INVOICE	TERMS	P.R.	PURCHASES DEBIT	OTHER ACCOUNTS DEBIT	ACCOUNTS PAYABLE CREDIT

Working Papers, Chapter 6　　　　　　　　　　　　　　　　　　　　　　　　　　　　　299

CHAPTER 6 PROBLEM 6-5 or 6-5A (Continued)

CASH RECEIPTS JOURNAL
Page 3

DATE	ACCOUNT CREDITED	EXPLANATION	P.R.	OTHER ACCOUNTS CREDIT	ACCOUNTS RECEIVABLE CREDIT	SALES CREDIT	SALES DISCOUNTS DEBIT	CASH DEBIT

CASH DISBURSEMENTS JOURNAL
Page 3

DATE	CH. NO.	PAYEE	ACCOUNT DEBITED	P.R.	OTHER ACCOUNTS DEBIT	ACCOUNTS PAYABLE DEBIT	PURCHASES DISCOUNTS CREDIT	CASH CREDIT

CHAPTER 6   PROBLEM 6-5 or 6-5A (Continued)   Name _____

GENERAL JOURNAL   Page 2

DATE	ACCOUNT TITLES AND EXPLANATION	P.R.	DEBIT	CREDIT

ACCOUNTS RECEIVABLE LEDGER

NAME   Mary Cortez
ADDRESS   615 First Street

DATE	EXPLANATION	P.R.	DEBIT	CREDIT	BALANCE

NAME   Dean Grammer
ADDRESS   1316 2nd Avenue North

DATE	EXPLANATION	P.R.	DEBIT	CREDIT	BALANCE

NAME   Tamara Smith
ADDRESS   1442 Beck Street

DATE	EXPLANATION	P.R.	DEBIT	CREDIT	BALANCE

CHAPTER 6   PROBLEM 6-5 or 6-5A (Continued)

ACCOUNTS PAYABLE LEDGER

NAME   Dunlap Company
ADDRESS   207 North 22nd Street

DATE	EXPLANATION	P.R.	DEBIT	CREDIT	BALANCE

NAME   Hollingsworth Company
ADDRESS   105 Central Avenue

DATE	EXPLANATION	P.R.	DEBIT	CREDIT	BALANCE

NAME   Riteway Company
ADDRESS   2711 Walnut

DATE	EXPLANATION	P.R.	DEBIT	CREDIT	BALANCE

NAME   The Store Depot
ADDRESS   137 Oak Street

DATE	EXPLANATION	P.R.	DEBIT	CREDIT	BALANCE

GENERAL LEDGER

Cash   Account No. 101

DATE	EXPLANATION	P.R.	DEBIT	CREDIT	BALANCE

CHAPTER 6 PROBLEM 6-5 or 6-5A (Continued) Name _____

Accounts Receivable — Account No. 106

DATE	EXPLANATION	P.R.	DEBIT	CREDIT	BALANCE

Office Supplies — Account No. 124

DATE	EXPLANATION	P.R.	DEBIT	CREDIT	BALANCE

Store Supplies — Account No. 125

DATE	EXPLANATION	P.R.	DEBIT	CREDIT	BALANCE

Office Equipment — Account No. 163

DATE	EXPLANATION	P.R.	DEBIT	CREDIT	BALANCE

Accounts Payable — Account No. 201

DATE	EXPLANATION	P.R.	DEBIT	CREDIT	BALANCE

Sales — Account No. 413

DATE	EXPLANATION	P.R.	DEBIT	CREDIT	BALANCE

Working Papers, Chapter 6

CHAPTER 6   PROBLEM 6-5 or 6-5A (Continued)

Sales Returns and Allowances — Account No. 414

DATE	EXPLANATION	P.R.	DEBIT	CREDIT	BALANCE

Sales Discounts — Account No. 415

DATE	EXPLANATION	P.R.	DEBIT	CREDIT	BALANCE

Purchases — Account No. 505

DATE	EXPLANATION	P.R.	DEBIT	CREDIT	BALANCE

Purchases Returns and Allowances — Account No. 506

DATE	EXPLANATION	P.R.	DEBIT	CREDIT	BALANCE

Purchases Discounts — Account No. 507

DATE	EXPLANATION	P.R.	DEBIT	CREDIT	BALANCE

Sales Salaries Expense — Account No. 621

DATE	EXPLANATION	P.R.	DEBIT	CREDIT	BALANCE

Advertising Expense — Account No. 655

DATE	EXPLANATION	P.R.	DEBIT	CREDIT	BALANCE

CHAPTER 6 PROBLEM 6-5 or 6-5A (Continued) Name _____

CHAPTER 6 PROBLEM 6-5 or 6-5A (Concluded)

CHAPTER 6   PROBLEM 6-6 or 6-6A   Name _____

CHAPTER 6   PROBLEM 6-7 or 6-7A   Name _____